D0894372

## Acknowledgements

Many thanks to my agent, Tony Peake, and to my editors David Reynolds and Monica Macdonald.

For their generosity and accessibility, I am indebted to James Grauerholz, Bob Rosenthal, Ira Silverberg, and the PEN Freedom-To-Write Committee.

For their nourishment and support: Jane Cheadle, Jo Frankham, Julie and David Hesmondhalgh, Anna Magyar, Maggie MacLure, Peter McConnell, Kolin O'Brien, and Duncan Webster.

This book is dedicated to Kathleen Caveney.

There are probably more generalizations about the differences between England and America than the actual differences themselves. They bombard us via TV cliché, anecdote and humor; discourses that blend prejudice with observation, abstract theory and personalized travelogue. The earnest American versus the ironic (pronounced "iron-ic") European, the Old World and the New. England did not just colonize America, she invented it – another chance at Eden, a dream through which, in the words of Fitzgerald, man could come "face to face for the last time in history with something commensurate to his capacity for wonder."

During the course of its great experiment, America re-invented the old world she had left behind, simultaneously glad to be free of its corruption while reluctantly acknowledging its allure. In his letters, Henry James was to write of "the difficulty of writing a romance about a country where there is no shadow, no antiquity, no mystery, no picturesque and gloomy wrong, nor anything but a commonplace prosperity, in broad and simple daylight as is happily the case with my dear native land." Innocent America may have been, but it was Europe who had the experience: the curse of God's Chosen was that they suspected it was the Devil who had the better tunes.

Between these two polarities a whole series of personal investments and cultural fantasies have been exchanged. For George Bernard Shaw the two cultures consisted of one people divided by a common language. D.H. Lawrence cast America as Europe's avenging infant, its literature being driven by the rage of Oedipal trauma. Most recently, the critic Jean Baudrillard has constructed America as a post-modern playpen, not so much a country as a collection of images, all reproducing themselves in promiscuous abandon: "America ducks the question of origins; it cultivates no origin or mythical authenticity; it has no past and no founding truth. Having known no primitive accumulation of time, it lives in a perpetual present."

I am not so much interested in the validity of these constructs as I am in their potency. That a culture's identity is imaginary does not necessarily make it any the less real. Indeed, one could argue that it makes it all the more so – a process of establishing "the facts" by examining the fictions that sustain them. It is within this framework – the binary of Europe and America – that I wish to introduce another set of oppositions. During the course of researching the life and work of Allen Ginsberg, it became clear that he raises yet another conversation between Europe and America: the confrontation between the biographer and the autobiographer.

In his classic novel of the 1880's, *Portrait of a Lady*, Henry James dramatizes an exchange that can be seen to encapsulate the divergent ways in which Americans and Europeans characterize their notions of Self. The following takes place between the duplicitous yet stately Mme. Merle and the naïve but spirited heroine Isabel Archer:

"'I don't care anything about this house,' said Isabel.

'That's very crude of you. When you've lived as long as I you'll see that every human being has his shell and that you must take the shell into account. By the shell I mean the whole envelope of circumstances. There's no such thing as an isolated man or woman; we're each of us made up of some cluster of appurtenances. What shall we call our 'self'? Where does it begin? Where does it end? It overflows into everything that belongs to us – and then it flows back again. I know a large part of myself is in the clothes I choose to wear. I've a great respect for things! One's self – for other people – is one's expression of one's self; and one's house, one's furniture, one's garments, the books one reads, the company one keeps – these things are all expressive.'"

Isabel's reply could well be inscribed on Ginsberg's tombstone:

" 'I don't agree with you. I think just the other way. I don't know whether I succeed in expressing myself, but I know that nothing else expresses me. Nothing that belongs to me is any measure of me; everything's on the contrary a limit, a barrier, and a perfectly arbitrary one. Certainly the clothes which, as you say, I choose to wear, don't express me; and heaven forbid they should!'

'You dress very well,' Madame Merle lightly interposed.

'Possibly; but I don't care to be judged by that. My clothes express the dressmaker, but they don't express me. To begin with it's not my own choice that I wear them; they're

Previous page: Ginsberg on board the *S.S. John Blair* in New York Harbor, 1947. (© Allen Ginsberg Trust.)
Overleaf: With Peter Orlovsky, Paris, 1956. Their partnership lasted more than thirty years. (© Topham.)

2

imposed upon me by society.'

'Should you prefer to go without them?' Madame Merle inquired in a tone which virtually terminated the discussion."

The point being, of course, that this does not terminate the discussion. For Ginsberg's answer, like so many American Selves, is a resounding "Yes!" Being naked, whether as metaphor or occasionally in his performances, is a testament to America's sanctity of the self. Clearly, the genre in which the Self is most fittingly celebrated is that of the autobiography; and for Ginsberg's work to be rescued from charges of self-absorption and confessional verse, he must first be located within a tradition that is as old as America itself, a tradition wherein Americans wrote using their experience not as private memoir but as public declaration. Ginsberg is a poet who denounces the world around him by placing his naked ego at the center of it, an accuser who was complicit with his own charges. In placing his queer shoulder to America's wheel, he forces us to consider the queerness of the wheel itself.

Before considering why Ginsberg's legacy survives, it is necessary to look briefly at what came before.


It is not unreasonable to assert that the founding father of American literature was autobiography itself. Of course, Europe also has its tradition of the genre – John Stuart Mill, Augustine, Rousseau, for example – but all these texts were written after the authors had reached some level of prominence and social-standing. What I would suggest is that, for the American, it was precisely through writing autobiography that such things were achieved. Mme. Merle's contention that the self is essentially a connected one seems anathema to a nation who believes not only in the self-made man, but also in the self-written one.

Autobiography is American ideology writ large.

From the very beginnings with the Puritan settlers, the writing of a conversion narrative was the key to forging a separate identity. The Puritans' covenant with God and country necessitated that they describe both their earlier debauchery and the moment of revelation that brought about their conversion. Figures such as Jonathon Edwards and John Winthrop did not write their autobiographies because of some national interest in

3

their personae, but rather as a means of constructing them.

Again, whereas eighteenth-century European narratives tended to be fictionalized biographies and autobiographies (Swift's "Gulliver," Fielding's "Tom Jones," Richardson's "Pamela"), America turned instead to the confessional tales of real-life conmen such as *The Memoirs of the Notorious Stephen Burroughs of New Hampshire* or to memoirs of captivity amongst the native Americans – John Hunter's journals being, perhaps, the most famous example. The list goes on. America's emphasis on self-reliance and rugged individualism finds its aesthetic voice in the (auto)biographies of Benjamin Franklin, Thoreau, Henry Adams and Norman Mailer. For all these writers, the Song is of Themselves. For Ralph Waldo Emerson, "There is no history; there is only Biography. We are very clumsy writers of history. The great value of Biography consists in the perfect sympathy that exists between like minds." Put another way, the individual is not a product of history, but its agent; the writing of their experience not a reflection on becoming, rather its very fabric – a (w)rite of passage, as it were.

To the self-effacing European, such an outline might sound like triumphalist chest-beating. Indeed, one could argue that it does not take much straining to hear Whitman's "Song of Myself" (I celebrate myself, and sing myself/And what I assume you shall assume) echoing through the villages of Vietnam. Yet it is worth remembering that American self-exposure has also opened up spaces in which competing voices can be heard, in which the self-composed subject serves as a damning acronym for its society. The slave narratives of Frederick Douglass

This page: With erstwhile lover Neal Cassady, San Francisco, 1954.
(© Allen Ginsberg Trust.) Overleaf: With Gary Snyder at the Human Be-In, San Francisco, 1967. (© Gene Anthony.)

and Harriet Jacobs can be read as testaments to the triumph of self-invention, but in so doing they provide accusatory evidence of the obstacles that have been placed in the way of that self-same journey. Their explanations of their own experience hold up a mirror to the same society that sought to deny the reality of such reflections.

The democratic promise held out by autobiography has received many unsolicited replies from a myriad of women writers – a lineage that stretches from Margaret Fuller and Sojourner Truth through to Maya Angelou and John Didion.

If one side of the American Self could be said to lead to Vietnam, the other takes us to the politicized prison memoirs of George Jackson and Alexander Berkman. As Macolm X succinctly put it: "If I honestly and fully tell my life's account, read objectively it might prove to be a testimony of social value . . . history may even say that my voice helped to save America from a grave, or fatal catastrophe."

Against this backdrop of radical selves, of aggressive egos and bruised solipsists, emerged Allen Ginsberg. His life transformed itself into poetry to the point of a Siamese connection – each taking its cue from the other. He flaunted his damage as America's own, measuring the health of the nation by the yardstick of his own psyche. His persona contained the multitudes of the culture, his repertoire of selves a reflection of America's multiple personalities. Ginsberg's candor about his inner world serves as a public critique, allowing him to point the finger at America by pointing it at himself.

If Ginsberg's self embraces various (United) States, what then are the contours of its topography? Firstly there is his Jewishness, as indelible a part of his identity as circumcision. Ginsberg offers us the cultural archetypes of the Jew as Intellectual and as "macher," representing in turn those semi-stereotypes of excessive ambition and pensive introspection respectively. Even in its secularity, Ginsberg the intellectual Jew manifests itself in his sense of literary vocation. The sheer volume of material that he produced (journals and essays as well as poetry) reveals a mind that was inexhaustibly enquiring.

Relentlessly productive, Ginsberg perversely displayed a version of the exemplary literary life. His infamous scrawling of "FUCK THE JEWS" on his Columbia room window only serves to inscribe him further into his heritage – a kind of Jewish joke whose punchline is confrontationally ambiguous. As Irving Howe pointedly wrote: "We might scorn our origins; we might crush America with discoveries of ardor; we might change our

names. But we knew that but for an accident of geography we might also now be bars of soap . . . Our Jewishness might have no clear religious or national content, it might be helpless before the criticism of believers; but Jews we were, like it or not, and liked or not."

Contrasted with the studious urban Jew, there exists Ginsberg the meditative Buddhist – the man who sought a transcendent serenity through the sonority of mantra. If his Jewishness taught him the importance of resistance, his Buddhism offered him a cite of surrender – a religion of calm passivity as opposed to that of suspicious self-preservation. The Columbia student who defiantly exposed the anti-Semitism of his university is the same man who chose acquiescence when mugged on the streets of Manhattan: "I went down shouting Om Ah Hum to gangs of lovers on the stoop watching."

For a poet so haunted by the specter of destruction, Ginsberg refused to succumb to

Ginsberg at Auschwitz. His Jewishness was an indelible part of his personality, though perhaps an ambiguous one. (© Allen Ginsberg Trust.)

his own doomed prophecies. He may have seen "the best minds of my generation destroyed by madness," but, ultimately, he was not to be one of them. In his classic novel *Humboldt's Gift*, Saul Bellow has written of how America "is proud of its dead poets. It takes terrific satisfaction in the poet's testimony that the USA is too tough, too big, too much, too rugged, that American reality is overpowering. And to be a poet is a school thing, a skirt thing, a church thing. The weakness of the spiritual powers is proved in the childishness, madness, drunkenness, and despair of these martyrs . . . So poets are loved, but loved because they just can't make it here." While Ginsberg's poetry appears to concur with Bellow's rule, his life proved to be its exception. Despite his sectionings and hallucinations, Ginsberg lived to the age of seventy – a peaceful death that sabotaged the image of Romantic self-ruin.

Unlike the burned-out euphoria of his predecessors – Hart Crane, Randall Jarrell, John Berryman – Ginsberg was just simply too ironic to join the ranks of the beautiful but the damned. Even, or especially within his most tortured visions, there remains a quality of self-mockery, an ability to satirize his own suffering even as he weeps. It is a gift that he himself described as belonging to "The trickster-hero . . . that question 'twixt earnest and joke." Sincerity for Ginsberg is always accompanied by a touch of the absurd. He ridicules his anguish as though he were Lear and his fool incarnated as one.

In her thrilling study of "American Humor: A Study of the National Character," Constance Rourke wrote of how the Puritan heritage had made it necessary for Americans to adopt a mask. Authenticity was not something to be opposed to artifice, but rather a range of emotions to be etched upon it. As Rourke writes, "In a primitive world crowded with pitfalls, the unchanging, unaverted countenance had been a safeguard, preventing revelations of surprise, anger, or dismay. The mask had otherwise become habitual among the older Puritans as their more expressive or risible feelings were sunk beneath the surface . . . No doubt the mask would prove useful in a country where the Puritan was still a power and the risks of pioneering by no means over." The ironic ring to Ginsberg's emotional extremes is the mask through which he shows us his face, demonstrating, as Wilde might say, that natural feelings are a most difficult pose to maintain.

Perhaps the most striking example of Ginsberg's fluidity is to be found in his involvement with the Beats. On the one hand, he is such an exemplar of the beaten-yet-beatific poet to almost be its caricature. He stares out at us like a figure from the Old Testament – the wild-haired bearded prophet, lost in the wilderness of his own lyrical musings. His appearance tells us that he is not of this world, but belongs instead to some mystical land which can be discovered only through hallucinations and the secrets of William Blake. On the other, he was the most worldly of the Beats, constantly hustling on their behalf, acting as unofficial agent, editor and publicist. Whilst Burroughs was strung out in Tangier, it was Ginsberg who persuaded Ace Books to publish *Junkie* and who went on to help persuade Olympia Press to take on *The Naked Lunch*. He was similarly supportive of Kerouac, and could arguably be said to be responsible for making *On the Road* the cult-classic that it has become.

From New York to San Francisco, Ginsberg seems to have been a facilitator of poetry as well as a practitioner. His work may have recklessly patrolled the negroid streets, but another side of him was the arch entrepreneur. As Jane Kramer said of him: "One of his friends has called Ginsberg the central casting office of the underground. He enters the name, address, and phone number of anyone he meets who plays, or is apt to play, a part in what he thinks of as the new order – or has information that might be useful to it – in the address book that he always carries in his purple bag, and he goes to considerable trouble putting people he likes in touch with each other and with sympathetic and influential Establishment characters who might be helpful to them. In this way, Ginsberg has managed to create a network of the like-minded around the world. Any one of his friends who goes to a city that Ginsberg has ever visited knows in advance where to stay, whom to see, and what local statutes to avoid breaking, not to mention who the local shamen are, what politicians are friendly, who has bail money, who sells pot, the temperament of the chief of police, the sympathies of the editors of all the newspapers, the phone numbers of the local activists, and where the best sex and the best conversation can be found."

Again, Ginsberg's role as cultural switchboard has its roots in an American tradition that stretches from W.D. Howells's championing of younger writers through Pound's support of Eliot to the encouragement of new writers such as Jay McInerney by the likes of Raymond Carver. Ginsberg's impact is to be found not just in his verse, but also in the broader context of cultural intervention.

This sense of being engaged in every aspect of literary production may be just one of the reasons that Ginsberg also cast himself in the role of political activist. Considering they were "The Only Rebellion Around," the Beats were surprisingly reticent in their politics. Burroughs may have been obsessed with systems of control, but his position was ultimately one of *laissez-faire* individualism. Despite his dabblings in Buddhism, Kerouac never really shook off the strictures of his Catholicism and reacted to the radicalism of the sixties with a mixture of contempt and a depressing sense  that he had been horribly misread by its children. Cassady was always too much the Wild One to ever ally himself to any ideology, while Hunke's eternal hustling made him a perverse version of the self-made man.

Existential hedonism is perhaps the closest one can come to characterizing the Beat

With William S. Burroughs, Jean Genet and Dick Seaver at the Chicago Democratic Convention, 1968. (© Fred W. McDarrah.)

At home in Paterson with
his father, Louis.
(© Elsa Dorfman.)

politic – a philosophy that rebelled in its inner world and was driven purely by the imperatives of the moment. Norman Mailer would later reflect that, "The common denominator for all of them is their burning consciousness of the present, exactly that incandescent consciousness which the possibilities within death has opened for them. There is a depth of desperation to the condition which enables one to remain in life only by engaging in death, but the reward is their knowledge that what is happening at each instant of the electric present is good or bad for them, good or bad for their causes, their love, their action, their need."

Yet Ginsberg never lost sight of the outer world. His parents had been communist and socialist and he had entertained fantasies of becoming a labor lawyer and fighting the good fight. The prosecution of "Howl" re-affirmed him in his belief that the poetic was also the political. Throughout the sixties he became a key player in the anti-war movement, most famously at the Democratic Convention of 1968. In the eighties he travelled to Nicaragua in support of the Sandinista government, and in the nineties would reflect that a pivotal question still remains: "Who owns all the money? Who owns the media? . . . In America it's only twenty-two people who own 80% of the mass media. It would be very difficult for a poet to overcome that barrage of bullshit. On the other hand, poetry is the only place where you get an individual person telling his subjective truth, what he really thinks as opposed to what he wants people to think he thinks – like a politician or an editorial . . . So you have to follow Shelley in that poets are the unacknowledged legislators of the race. Or what William Carlos Williams said more acutely, 'the government is of words.'

"After all," he continued, "people making political speeches, they're writing prose if not poetry. They're trying to get a little flowery language in there, but the language is shifty and the language is manipulative and peoplewho are in advertising or the mass media can't say what they really think. But the poet can say what he really thinks authentically, and that's the advantage. And it's longer lasting than the immediate radio or television broadcast 'cos a poem is like a radio that can broadcast for thousands of years. So in the long run, poetry may still have an ameliorating effect on the spirit."

For many of the Beat writers, poetry was a way of constructing alternative worlds. For Ginsberg, it was a means of talking back to this one.

And then there is the sex. Desperate, euphoric, defiant, aggressive, masochistic, celebratory descriptions of his homosexual encounters. His Hell's Angels, his supermarket boys, his child hoods, his masters and his slaves – Ginsberg brings a whole new meaning to the concept of the oral tradition. What are we to make of his phallus-worship, his notches on the bed-post in cock-sure verse? One context in which this could be placed could be provided by the work of the critic Leslie A. Fiedler. In his classic study "Love and Death in the American Novel," he argues that the canon of American fiction is driven by the homoerotic, of love, in Hemingway's phrase, of "men without women". Jay Gatsby and Nick Carraway, Ishmael and Queequeg, Huck Finn and Jim, Natty Bumbo and Chingachgook, the Lone Ranger and Tonto – American fiction is the attempt to free its

A poetry reading
in Washington State
Park, N.Y.C., 1966.
(© Charles Gatewood.)

men from their women and provide them with a setting in which homosocial romance can flourish.

"Where woman is felt to be a feared and forbidden other," writes Fiedcr, "the only legitimate beloved is the self. Pure narcissism cannot, however, provide the dream and tension proper to a novel; the mirror-image of the self is translated in the American novel . . . into the comrade of one's own sex, the buddy as *anima* . . . Marriage to a woman would have seemed to Melville's hero intolerable; only through a pure wedding of male to male could he project an engagement with life which did not betray the self.

"This is an alternative deeply appealing to the American mind and essentially congenial to the American experience."

This was clearly the case for the Beats, Dean Moriarty and Sal Paradise being the most striking example. What Ginsberg achieves through his litany of experiences is to take America's homoeroticism at its word. His promotion of the "boy-gang" as the most fitting foundation for literature exposes an attitude that is already latent yet central to American culture. Melville, Twain, Hemingway et al were writing homoeroticism within a heterosexual framework. Ginsberg takes their subtexts and puts them on display – a kind of literary "outgoing," as it were. Men without women suggests an absence – Ginsberg replaces it with his presence.

Ginsberg carved out a protean Self, an autobiographical mask that had many guises and spoke with many voices: the Buddhist-Jew, the political Beat, the entrepreneurial mystic, the traditional dissident, the ironic confessor – he brought such binaries together, in order that they may fall apart.

Echoing the maxim of his hero, Walt Whitman:

Do I contradict myself?
Very well then . . . I contradict myself
I am large . . . I contain multitudes

Ginsberg offers us an identity that is as in conflict as his culture. As he so succinctly expressed it himself,

It occurs to me that I am America.
I am talking to myself again.

It is the interaction between the two statements – the poetic logic that leads us from one to the other – that gave Ginsberg's project its urgency and appeal, that places the dialogue between his disparate selves so deeply within the American grain.

Chapter

1

Previous page: Ginsberg
with his parents, Naomi
and Louis, 1939.
(© Allen Ginsberg Trust.)

Allen Ginsberg's family was the product of enforced flight and chosen exile, their story reading like the plot of some nineteenth-century naturalist novel. His maternal grandparents hailed from a Jewish quarter near St. Petersburg, a small town called Nevel. His grandfather, Mendel Livergant, ran a sewing-machine business there and embodied the distinctly Eastern European combination of business acumen and deep-seated radicalism. His wife, Judith, shared his revolutionary sympathies, and it was these that prompted them to flee from the pro-Czarist Russo-Japanese War of 1904, and join the flux of émigrés to America. At Ellis Island, Mendel Livergant became Morris Levy. The art of re-invention was to be a family heirloom.

Ginsberg's paternal grandparents followed a similar path, although one taken more voluntarily. Pinkus opted for Newark over his native Warsaw in the 1880s, and it was here that he met his wife, Rebecca, who had made a similar crossing from the Ukraine a decade earlier.

Given such backgrounds, as well as New Jersey's noble labor history, it was inevitable that their children would be raised in the traditions of the Left. Ginsberg's father, Louis, was reared on the

Ginsberg's maternal grandparents,
Mendel and Judith Levy (center).
Their shared political sympathies
prompted their move from Russia
to the U.S.A. in 1904.
(© Allen Ginsberg Trust.)

Ginsberg's paternal grandfather, Pinkus, met his wife Rebecca when he moved to Newark from Warsaw in the 1880s. (© Allen Ginsberg Trust.)

politics of the Wobblies and tales of John Reed. His mother, Naomi, like her sister, became a card-carrying member of the Communist Party. Louis and Naomi were married in 1919. Two distinct yet complementary aspects of Ginsberg's character can be seen in his parents. Louis was the personification of stability, a man who taught English for forty years at the Central High School in Paterson. He was also a lyric poet of no small standing, his work appearing throughout the twenties in *The New Masses, The New York Times* and various anthologies of contemporary verse. His work was conventional in its attention to meter, rhyme and conceit – New Jersey's A.E. Houseman – and yet it was respected as competent if not inspired. Ginsberg has acknowledged his father's influence, recalling that he "learnt the art of lyric – which comes from the stringed instrument lyre – at his knee when I was five years old as his apprentice. There's a family business here. He wrote a number of very beautiful poems that I've echoed, especially in 'Father Death Blues.'"

Naomi and Louis, Ginsberg's parents, 1917, two years before their marriage. (© Allen Ginsberg Trust.)

Louis taught at Paterson Central High School for forty years, but was also a poet – the man from whom Ginsberg "learnt the art of the lyric." (© Allen Ginsberg Trust.)

Father and son could not have been further apart in terms of technique, aesthetics or poetic purpose. Yet Ginsberg remained his father's son in his commitment to the idea of writing as a vocation; for literature to be engaged.

But it was to his mother and her madness that Ginsberg was born on June 3, 1926. She had already suffered a nervous breakdown seven years earlier while working as a school teacher, her symptoms manifesting themselves as a paralysing sensitivity to any light or sound. It was a pattern that was to re-occur with depressing regularity. Even at the age of three, Ginsberg was visiting his mother at the Bloomingdale Sanatorium. Her illness ranged from persecution and paranoia to depression and dementia. At times she was convinced that her mother-in-law was trying to poison her, at others that President Roosevelt had placed wires in her head in order to access her private thoughts. She was institutionalized for three years during her son's adolescence, only to return with amnesia due to a cocktail of ECT, Metrasol and insulin-shock treatment. She would often be found naked wandering through the streets – an image that would clearly haunt her son's later work.

Towards the end of his life, Ginsberg recalled the distress felt by all parties concerned: "In the thirties I remember visiting her in sanatoriums . . . and as I grew up I had to take care of her when I was nine, ten, thirteen. I visited her by myself in mental hospitals that were grimy, huge, drab prisons." Perhaps the most disturbing factor of all was that it was to Ginsberg that the doctors turned for a signature on the consent form for a lobotomy: "I was told that she was in a state of such paroxysm, high blood pressure, anguish, banging her head literally bloody against the wall, that if I didn't take action, that I had to sign, she would have had a stroke. And rather naïvely believing what they had to say I signed. So I've always felt an enormous guilt and uncertainty about it."

Between the paternalistic professionalism of his father and the erratic despair of his mother, Ginsberg fluctuated with a nervous unease. His point of identification was with both, adopting a fatherly concern towards his mother, while experiencing her instability as his possible birthright. As he was to put it, "I had to deal with her irrationality, but as a kid not knowing if it was irrational or real. I had to deal with it diplomatically. It gave me a lot of armory."

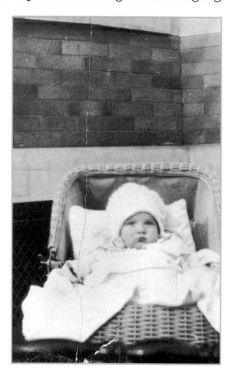

Allen Ginsberg was born on June 3, 1926. (© Allen Ginsberg Trust.)

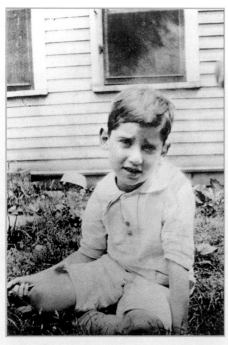

Eugène Ginsberg, Allen's
older brother, 1930.
(© Allen Ginsberg Trust.)

For many poets of moon-struck Romance, madness operates as a melodramatic pose – a convenient metaphor for dramatizing their alienation from the world. For Ginsberg, however, such clichés have an empirical urgency to them. They are not just a part of his literary personae, they are the brutal truths of his personal landscape.

Emotional cost aside, Naomi's mental illness proved to be an expensive affliction, especially during the Depression of the thirties. Louis had to borrow heavily from the Credit Union to pay for his wife's care, eventually owing $3,600 – the equivalent of a year's salary. He was also forced to rely on a network of family and friends to feed and look after Allen and his older brother, Eugène.

Hardship served to further politicize the Ginsbergs: holidays at Communist summer camps, Naomi becoming the branch secretary of the local Party Cell, Louis continuing in the class struggle of socialism. The Depression led to contradictory responses in the

As a young boy, Ginsberg was bespectacled, toothbraced, bookish, and shy. (© Allen Ginsberg Trust.)

American psyche. One reaction was to internalize social failures as personal shortcomings. American ideology had long lent itself to the impression that there was no such thing as a system, but only individuals. (Naturally, when the system failed, those individuals had no one to blame but themselves. The popularity of the game Monopoly, a bi-product of the Crash of 1929, was both a celebration and a critique of how capitalism conflated personal choice with random chance.) Alternatively, the sheer scale of the Depression necessitated mobilization – the acknowledgement that social pressures were weighing more heavily on the population than mere self-reliance could cope with. The Jeffersonian cry, "That government is best which governs least," was not a philosophy that could accommodate the stark fact of twenty-five million unemployed.

It was as though in her illness and in her politics Naomi embodied both responses. While one side of herself withdrew into the darker recesses of her mind, the other confronted the political realities that it had forced it into hiding. The Madwoman in the Party thus becomes a potent symbol – a figure who is martyr and agitator, symptom and solution both. Hence in

This page: Ginsberg saw his mother's instability as a possible birthright, "not knowing if it was real." (© Allen Ginsberg Trust.) Overleaf: Family vacations were often taken at Communist summer camps. (© Allen Ginsberg Trust.)

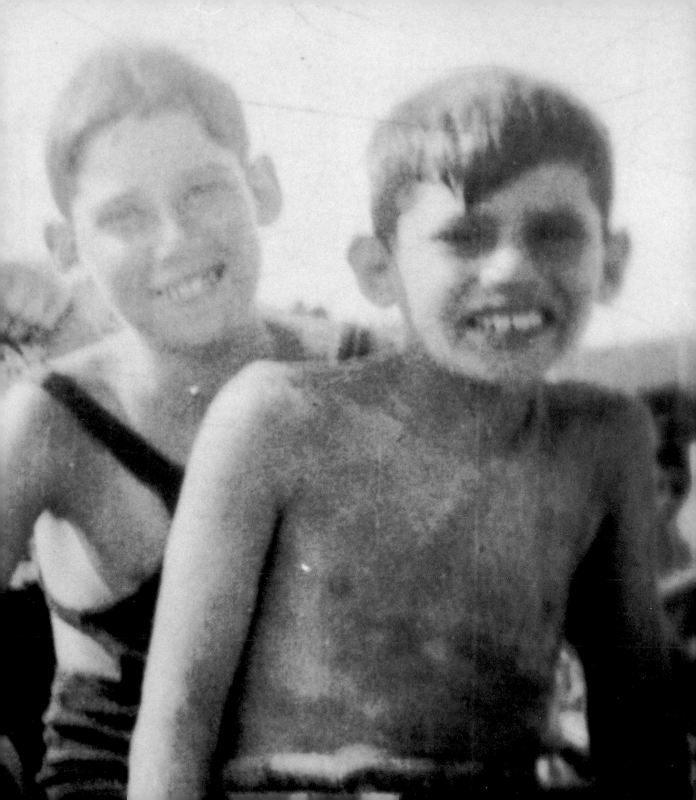

Mendel Levy (left) with the
Ginsbergs, 1933.
(© Allen Ginsberg Trust.)

"America," Ginsberg was able to wax lyrical about the "momma [who] took me to Communist Cell meetings . . . and the speeches were free everybody was angelic and sentimental about the workers it was all so sincere you have no idea what a good thing the party was," while lamenting in the poem "Kaddish," "Naomi, Naomi – sweating, bulge-eyed, fat, the dress un-buttoned at one side – hair over brow, her stocking hanging evilly on her legs – screaming for a blood transfusion." His mother was not simply a member from his childhood, but a woman whose schizophrenia mirrored America's divided self.

In 1934 the family moved to 155 Haledon Avenue, and, two years later, two blocks down to number 72. During this time, Ginsberg was living out to the letter the script of the introverted schoolboy. Bespectacled, wearing tooth-braces, crippled by same-sex crushes, bullied, bookish and shy – his pre-pubescence reads like a Woody Allen routine, but without the punch-line. His mother's condition erupted sporadically, making home as fraught a place as school. The hospitalizations continued, precipitating feelings of both abandonment and relief in her youngest son. He did find some refuge in the darkness of the movie theatre, and would later poeticize the cinema as a comforting dreamscape. Yet he was a desperate boy, someone he would remember later as "A kind of mental ghoul, totally disconnected from any reality, existing in a world of newspapers and aesthetics."

Ginsberg graduated from grammar school on June 27, 1939, by which time his family had moved again, this time to 288 Graham Avenue in downtown Paterson. In his yearbook he named Poe as his favorite writer, and proclaimed that his motto was, "Do what you want to when you want to." He moved on to Central High in 1940, and began to emerge from his shell via his interest in English and involvement in the school magazine. A year later he moved to East Side High, emersing himself in student drama and the debating society. It was here that he was first introduced to the work of Walt Whitman – a significant encounter which would only be appreciated retrospectively.

At the age of sixteen, Ginsberg enrolled with Civilian Defense, spending evenings on patrol duty as well as waging a letter-writing campaign against the isolationists. The "Do what you want to when you want to" maxim may have been the quip of a flippant adolescent, but the passion with which the young Ginsberg urged America to enter the war against fascism suggests a much more passionate and earnest radical.

It was with all this blossoming sincerity that Ginsberg prepared to enter Columbia University.

**Ginsberg graduated from East Side High, Paterson, in June 1943, and prepared himself for Columbia University.**
**(© Allen Ginsberg Trust.)**

Chapter

2

**This and previous page:
Ginsberg began his studies at
Columbia with a strong sense
of commitment to idealism
shared with his parents.
(© Allen Ginsberg Trust.)**

When Ginsberg began his studies at Columbia, he did so with the same commitment to idealism as his parents had. Preparing to further the struggle by working within the Labor movement, he studied economics and politicized the debating society. Yet it was the English department that enchanted him during his freshman year. Raymond Weaver, Melville's biographer, taught there, as did the poet and critic Mark Van Doren, a Pulitzer prize-winner who was also the literary editor of the cultural magazine *The Nation.*

The most significant figure for Ginsberg, however, was undoubtedly Lionel Trilling. Trilling was a Jewish-American equivalent of F.R. Leavis – a deeply moral scholar who believed in the eternal verities of poetry and literature's great traditions. Diana, Trilling's wife, has characterized Ginsberg's relationship to her husband as a quasi-Oedipal struggle: "the wish to shock his teacher, and the wish to meet the teacher on equal ground . . . to propose an alliance between the views of the academic and the poet-rebel, the unity of a deep discriminating commitment to literature which must certainly one day wipe out the fortuitous distance between boy and man, pupil and teacher."

Another student of Trilling's was Lucien Carr, a blond boy from St. Louis with an ambitious intellect who was two years Ginsberg's senior. The two students shared the same halls at 122nd Street and Broadway, and Carr quickly became Ginsberg's first soul-mate, certainly his first Columbia crush.

Carr's boyish beauty had also captured the heart of an older man, David Kammerer, also from a respectable St. Louis background. Kammerer had become so infatuated with Carr that he had followed him from school to school, to the University of Chicago and now to New York. Carr found Kammerer's attention by turns

Ginsberg shared halls with Lucien Carr (center), who was his first soul-mate. Through Carr's friend David Kammerer, Ginsberg met the thirty-year-old William S. Burroughs. (© Allen Ginsberg Trust.)

flattering and irritating, attempting to maintain his friendship while keeping his sexual distance.

Back in St. Louis, Kammerer had been friends with William Burroughs, and it was on a visit to Kammerer's apartment at 69 Bedford St. that Ginsberg and Carr first met the thirty-year-old Burroughs. Ginsberg, still sweet-seventeen, was intrigued by the older man's air of worldly wisdom and keen intellect. During their first conversation, Burroughs casually quoted Shakespeare. Ginsberg remained largely silent, but equally impressed.

Ginsberg's initial self-image as the working class hero was gradually being displaced by that of the artisan poet. Rimbaud begins to replace Marx in his journals, and Verlaine starts making more sense than Engels. Carr and his girlfriend, Celine Young, Kammerer and Ginsberg made an ambiguous foursome, acting out their self-styled bohemianism in the bars around Columbia.

Their favorite haunt was the West End Bar, and it was here that Carr met Edie Parker and her boyfriend, an ex-Columbia football player, Jack Kerouac. Sensing that Ginsberg would appreciate his new drinking partner, Carr gave him Kerouac's address and encouraged him

**Ginsberg was intrigued by Burroughs's wisdom and intellect, and the older man soon became a mentor and sounding board for ideas. (© Charles Gatewood.)**

34

Ginsberg met Edie Parker (left) and her boyfriend, Jack Kerouac, in the West End Bar. (© Allen Ginsberg Trust.)

to pay a visit. In his autobiographical novel *Vanity of Duloz*, Kerouac wrote, "I was sitting in Edie's apartment one day when the door opened and in walks this spindly Jewish kid with horn-rimmed glasses and tremendous ears sticking out, seventeen years old, burning black eyes, a strangely deep voice." Ginsberg in turn recalled, "a big strong intelligent-looking football player merchant seaman . . . we talked and we discovered we both realized we were both on earth only temporarily. So there was a kind of understanding of the flowerness of the moment, a phrase of the day that we used."

It was the summer of 1944, and the nucleus of the Beat generation was beginning to take shape. The Kerouac–Carr–Ginsberg axis began to talk of a "New Vision" that would celebrate what Ginsberg's journals refer to as "the most individual, uninfluenced, unrepressed, uninhibited expression of art." Burroughs had been adopted as an off-the-wall mentor – a

Ginsberg saw Kerouac as "a big strong intelligent-looking football player merchant seaman." (© Allen Ginsberg Trust.)

sounding board for ideas, an antidote to their naïvety and an alternative librarian. Indeed, it was through Burroughs that the three young men were introduced to the works of Celine, Kafka, Baudelaire, Hart Crane and, perhaps most significantly for Ginsberg, William Blake.

As the group were brought closer together, they also fell apart. Kammerer's obsession with Carr began to take on shades of the psychotic: he was effectively stalking the young man, threatening his girlfriend, haunting his every footstep, breaking into his room to watch him sleep.

On August 14, 1944, Carr and Kammerer got drunk in the West End, then proceeded to take a bottle to Riverside Park. A drunken argument ensued, with Kammerer threatening to kill Carr and himself if he could not have Carr. When he tried to force himself on Carr, the younger man drew a pocket knife and stabbed Kammerer twice through the heart. He dumped the body in the Hudson and fled. He went first to see Burroughs who lent him some money and advised him to turn himself in, and then on to

Kerouac, and the two men went drinking around Times Square.

Two days later Carr went to the police, but they refused to believe his story. It was only later that day, when Kammerer's body was found floating by a coast-guard, that Carr was charged with murder and taken to Manhattan's jail. In the words of *The New York Times*: "The fantastic story of a homicide, first revealed to the authorities by the voluntary confession of a nineteen-year-old Columbia sophomore, was converted yesterday from a nightmarish fantasy into a horrible reality by the discovery of the bound and stabbed body of the victim in the murky waters of the Hudson River."

Carr pleaded guilty to second-degree manslaughter, citing the mitigating circumstances of Kammerer's infatuation.

With sobering reality, the "New Vision" of the group had been shown to have a murderous edge – their *laissez-faire* hedonism becoming re-cast as desperate tragedy. Even though it was Kerouac and Burroughs who had been arrested as material witnesses, Ginsberg was perhaps the most profoundly affected. At eighteen, he had none of the bitter-street experience of the others, and Carr's defence could not have but troubled someone who was himself still wrestling with homosexual crushes. "Everything I have loved of the past year has fled into the past," he wrote in his journals, and certainly the

Previous page: By the summer of
1944 the Beat generation began
to take shape – Hal Chase,
Kerouac, Ginsberg, and
Burroughs at Columbia.
(© Allen Ginsberg Trust.)

Ginsberg moved into
419 West 115th Street.
(© Bill Morgan.)

whole episode forced him to reflect not only on his alienation from the mainstream world, but also from the marginalized one of his new-found family.

After the trauma of the Kammerer–Carr case, Ginsberg found himself drawn much closer to Kerouac, who briefly moved in with him at Warren Hall. One night Ginsberg came out to him and was met by a groan: "It wasn't rejection," said Ginsberg, "It was a groan of dismay." Columbia University was nervous about this friendship – it was still smarting from the wounds that Carr had inflicted on its reputation, and it remembered Kerouac as a loutish jock. Ginsberg was advised to move on to campus at Livingstone Hall. Ironically, this made things worse, as Kerouac's visits now seemed clandestine. One night, after a long conversation about his problems with Edie, Kerouac stayed over. The arrangement was strictly chaste (Kerouac insisted on it), but they were awakened in the morning by the assistant dean of the university. The following day Ginsberg was fined for entertaining an unauthorized guest. This incident would not have been so damaging if it were not for the fact that Ginsberg had been writing graffiti on his windows. Convinced that his cleaning lady was an anti-Semite, he had scrawled "FUCK THE JEWS" in the dust of his windowpane. Lionel Trilling, the first Jew in the faculty, refused to see the irony in it, and, after an uncomfortable discussion, Ginsberg was expelled. Over a decade

later, he would return to Columbia to read his poetry – this time his homosexuality would be more than just rumored, and his obscenities more purposefully defiant.

He moved from

Ginsberg (second row from back, third in) joined the Navy for a three-month stint in 1945.
(© Allen Ginsberg Trust.)

SECTION 408
U.S. MARITIME SERVICE TRAINING STATION
SHEEPSHEAD BAY, BROOKLYN, N.Y.
AUG. 8. 1945

Livingstone into 419 West 115th St., in an apartment he shared with Jack and Edie Kerouac (who had married in August 1944), Joan Vollmer and her daughter, and a student called Hal Chase. Burroughs would join them later the same year. Ginsberg odd-jobbed for a while, working as a welder then a dishwasher. At the beginning of August 1945, he enrolled in the Navy out of the desperate need for money. His three-month stint was spent mainly in the sick-bay – a place where he could read Dostoevsky and recover from pneumonia. He emerged in November a few pounds lighter and $100 richer, and headed straight back to New York and the "New Visions."

Ginsberg returned to an apartment that was descending into disarray – a mixture of

creative chaos and drug-induced delusions – a time that Kerouac described as one "of evil decadence." Joan Vollmer had developed an insatiable appetite for Benzedrine. She would crack open nasal-inhalers and eat the "benny strips" inside. One strip would keep you going for eight hours; Joan was consuming at least four a day. Kerouac shared her enthusiasm to

Introduced to the Columbia group by Burroughs, Herbert Huncke represented the exotic allure of the criminal underworld.
(© Allen Ginsberg Trust.)

the point that his hair was beginning to fall out, and he had to apply make-up to disguise his wasted complexion. Burroughs by this time had discovered "junk" (heroin) and would spend entire days staring at the sole of his shoe. Paranoia abounded, with Joan particularly susceptible to what Burroughs simply termed "The Fear." She would move from being intelligent and lucid to believing that her neighbors were plotting to kill her or that all her male friends were out to rape her. By the end of 1946, she was admitted to Bellevue Hospital suffering from acute speed psychosis.

A key player in this turmoil had been Herbert Huncke, a seasoned Times Square hustler whom Burroughs had introduced to the Columbia circle. While they had previously been experimenting with drugs, Huncke introduced them to the life-style that accompanied them. He had left home when he was twelve and had learned every kind of hustle – from prescription forging to prostitution – on his way to New York. For the WASP-ish Burroughs and the Catholic Kerouac, Huncke represented the exotic allure of the criminal underworld. He was the "White Negro" before the term had been invented, and the man from whom Kerouac first heard the term "Beat." Huncke often used 115th St. to fence stolen goods, and in return he gave them an education of the streets, bringing the ethos of 42nd St. to the bookish world of the Upper West Side. If the apartment was on the verge of ordinary madness to begin with, Huncke was just the person to take it over the edge.

The energy that was generated by this turmoil appealed to Ginsberg, especially after the sterile confines of the Navy. He agreed to undergo psychoanalysis from Burroughs – every day they would embark on free association for one hour – Burroughs also introduced the household to "routines" – a role-playing game in which each person would act out different characters: a lesbian governess, a Southern tobacco farmer, an aristocratic Hungarian – all would make regular appearances.

On the down side, Ginsberg was in love with Kerouac. They had had a mutual masturbation encounter before he joined the navy. Indeed, much of Ginsberg's unhappiness in the services was due to love-sickness, his letters to Kerouac displaying all the intense yearning of unrequited desire. Kerouac was never comfortable in exploring his homosexuality: as Ginsberg said, "It was a very ambivalent relationship of him sort of denying interest but allowing it."

Despite the group's tempestuous appeal, it was obvious that the dynamics could not be sustained. Ginsberg decided to re-apply to Columbia, the earnest academic side of him never having been overshadowed by the rebellious poet. The dean would agree

William Cannastra (right) was a notorious, decadent party-giver and involved with the Beats until his accidental death in 1950. (© Allen Ginsberg Trust.)

only on condition that he got a letter from a psychiatrist. His mother's old doctor agreed to put a signature to the recommendation that Ginsberg had written himself. Not surprisingly, the evaluation concluded that "he is psychologically pretty much as sound as they come." Ginsberg was accepted for re-admission for the September term of 1946.

His timing could not have been better. Huncke had moved permanently into Hal Chase's now vacant room, and in April Burroughs was arrested for forging prescriptions. Huncke was then busted for possession, and Joan was already hospitalized.

Ginsberg closed down the apartment and wisely retreated back to Paterson to stay with his father.

Chapter

3

Previous page: Ginsberg on
the roof of his East Village
apartment, 1953.
(© Allen Ginsberg Trust.)

"Things going ill; poetry stopped, reading desultory, neurasthenic sleeping, loneliness, splenetic moods, boredom, fear, vanity." Thus did Ginsberg characterize his life three months after re-entering Columbia. Kerouac was back at his mother's writing, and Ginsberg was never invited owing to her virulent anti-Semitism. Burroughs was pot-farming in Texas, and Carr had come out of prison a changed man. Ginsberg compensated by drifting – socially, sexually and intellectually. He was still out of sorts with Trilling and Van Doren, and found greater inspiration in marijuana and Benzedrine.

He was rescued that winter by the arrival of Neal Cassady. Cassady – Dean Moriarty in *On The Road* – was born on February 8, 1926 in Salt Lake City, Utah. According to his autobiography, *The First Third*, he drifted with his alcoholic father through a series of dead-end jobs and two-bit motels. By the age of twenty-one, he had stolen more than 500 cars and served fifteen months in reform schools.

It was in Denver in 1945 that he met Hal Chase, who had returned home after his stay at 115th St. When Chase went back to Columbia, Cassady took the Greyhound to go and visit him. The New Visionaries immediately fell under his spell – seeing in his nomadic background an embodiment of their own saintly disaffection. As Kerouac wrote: "Dean's intelligence was . . . shining and complete, without the tedious intellectualness. And his

Ginsberg met Neal Cassady in 1946. "Two keen minds that they are, they took to each other at the drop of a hat," wrote Kerouac. (© Larry Keenan, Jr.)

'criminality' was not something that sulked and sneered; it was a wild yea-saying overburst of American joy; it was Western, the west wind, an ode from the Plains, something new, long prophesied, long-a-coming."

Kerouac was quick to sense the potential affinity of Ginsberg for his new friend, and introduced the two men early in 1946. Again, he records their meeting in *On The Road*: "Two keen minds that they are, they took to each other at the drop of a hat. Two piercing eyes glancing into two piercing eyes – the holy conman with the shining mind, and the sorrowful poetic conman with the dark mind . . . Their energies met head-on, I was a lout compared, I couldn't keep up with them."

Cassady and Ginsberg became lovers, an intense two-month affair in which Ginsberg felt himself dangerously enslaved by a man who prided himself on his heterosexual prowess. "I, somehow, dislike pricks & man & before you, had consciously forced myself to be homosexual," wrote Cassady. "I now feel I was forcing a desire for you bodily as a compensation to you for all you were giving me."

In 1947 Cassady fell in love with Carolyn Robinson, to whom he was later married. (© Allen Ginsberg Trust.)

Ginsberg had been due to visit him in Denver, and in July 1947 he made the trip by Greyhound, paid for by a writing competition he had won at Columbia. On his arrival, he found that Cassady was living with a Bennington girl called Carolyn Robinson, and relations became fraught with unspoken tensions for a time: Cassady was simultaneously getting divorced from his wife, LuAnne, and falling in love with Carolyn, and was now beginning to spurn Ginsberg's sexual demands. The more Ginsberg was rejected, the more obsessed he became, and his journals of the time are shot through with frustrated desire and jealous yearnings. He did, however, convince Cassady to take a trip with him to visit Burroughs in Texas.

Their visit was a vaudevillian mixture of Cassady chasing women and Ginsberg chasing Cassady, a kind of *Carry On Heartbeat* with a full supporting cast of Huncke, Vollmer and Burroughs.

In his frustration, Ginsberg took a ship out to Africa – a fifty-day round-trip in which he attempted to lose himself in the dope and the boys on offer there.

On returning to New York he rented a room on West 27th St. where he took lots of

Benzedrine and wrote rhyming couplets. He wrote regularly to Cassady, by turns accepting their break-up, then begging him to come back to him. Cassady failed to respond.

The next letter he received from Cassady would be to announce his marriage to Carolyn. Ironically it arrived on April 1. Ginsberg was furious: "I should congratulate you on your marriage. So O.K. Pops, everything you do is great. The idea of you with a child and settled center of attention – shit."

One positive result of his failed affair was that Ginsberg dedicated himself more to his work. "The Denver Doldrums" came out of this period, as did a frantic bout of reading and study.

By May 1948 Ginsberg was living at 321 East 121st St. in East Harlem. One day he was lying on his bed reading Blake's "Songs of Innocence and Experience." As he told it to the *Paris Review* in 1966: "As I often do, I had been jacking off while reading . . . And just after I came, on this occasion, with a Blake book on my lap – I wasn't even reading, my eye was over the page of 'Ah, Sun-flower,' and it suddenly appeared – the poem I'd read a lot of times before, overfamiliar to the

Having been rejected by Cassady, Ginsberg travelled to Dakar, West Africa, with the Merchant Marines in 1947.
(© Allen Ginsberg Trust)

Previous page: By 1949
Ginsberg was living on York
Avenue, where he found
himself babysitting Huncke.
(© Fred W. McDarrah.)

point where it didn't make any particular meaning except some sweet thing about flowers – and suddenly I realized the poem was talking about *me* . . . and suddenly, simultaneously with understanding it, I heard a very deep earthen voice in the room, which I immediately assumed, I didn't think twice, was Blake's voice . . . And my eye on the page, simultaneously the auditory hallucination . . . the apparitional voice in the room, woke me further deep in my understanding of the poem, because the voice was so completely tender and beautifully . . . ancient . . . I suddenly realized that *this* experience was *it!* And that I was born in order to experience up to this very moment that I was having this experience, to realize what this was all about – in other words that this was the moment that I was born for."

Ginsberg continues, recalling that Blake's voice then recited his poems "The Sick Rose" and "The Little Girl Lost." This mystical experience (schizophrenic delusion?) would alter the course of his life. He became obsessed with re-capturing the sensation, the insight, the communion with

During his hospitalization,
Ginsberg met wild child Carl
Solomon. He later dedicated
"Howl" to him.
(© Fred W. McDarrah.)

divinity. For the next fifteen years he would experiment with every mind-altering substance he could find in an attempt to re-live it.

The problem was trying to convince other people of what had happened without being seen as insane. His father's response was one of fear – that his wife's condition had been passed on to their son. The English faculty were no more understanding, and many of his teachers and friends advised him to see a psychiatrist.

Over the next year Ginsberg wrote at least nine poems about his epiphany, including "A Very Dove," "Do We Understand Each Other?," "The Voice of Rock," "A Western Ballad," and "On Reading William Blake's 'The Sick Rose.'" As late as 1986, Ginsberg would maintain that his vision was, "The only really genuine experience I feel I've had, something that seemed like a complete absorption of all my senses into something totally authentic."

Early in 1949 Ginsberg had moved to 1401 York Avenue where he found himself reluctantly baby-sitting Huncke, who had just been released from jail. Huncke parasitically exploited their friendship: he pawned Ginsberg's books and phonograph, feigned illness to generate sympathy, borrowed money he had no intention of re-paying and would spend days asleep on the couch as he came down from a Benzedrine binge.

Ginsberg's apartment became a dumping ground for stolen goods, Huncke's friends, Little Jack Melody and Vickie Russell, regularly off-loading hot items in Ginsberg's bedroom, until his patience finally snapped and he asked them to clear all their stolen gear out of his place. They arranged to do so and Ginsberg naïvely offered to help. Unaware that they were riding in a stolen car or that Little Jack had violated his parole, Ginsberg sat happily on the back seat surrounded by stolen clothes telling them about his trip to Africa. When a patrolman spotted them driving the wrong way up a one-way street, he signalled for them to pull over. The group panicked and a four-block car chase began that only ended when their car overturned. Although Ginsberg escaped back to his apartment, it was a matter of hours before he was arrested.

Trilling, Van Doren and Louis Ginsberg persuaded him to plead guilty and seek psychiatric help to avoid being sent to jail. With supporting testimony from his professors, Ginsberg was cleared, and on June 29, 1949 he was admitted to the sixth-floor ward of the Columbia Presbyterian Psychiatric Institute.

For the next seven months, Ginsberg's life would be subject to a strict régime of talking cures and close inspection. It was an institution in which "cure" was synonymous with conformity, and Ginsberg tried to co-operate. He played the part of the model patient in

In February 1950 Ginsberg
returned to Paterson to live
with his father and step-
mother, Edith.
(© Allen Ginsberg Trust.)

his sessions with the doctors, wisely keeping all talk of William Blake's voice to himself, and even went so far as to begin identifying with heterosexuality. Yet the most significant event of his hospitalization was his meeting a fellow-patient, Carl Solomon. Solomon was a Bronx-born wild child who allied himself with the avant-garde. He had been institutionalized for following the dictum of André Gide and performing "le crime gratuit." In his case it was stealing a peanut-butter sandwich and then showing it to a policeman. Ginsberg told him of his Blake vision, and Solomon in turn shared his life-story. Many of the episodes he related to Ginsberg would later become immortalized in "Howl," in addition to the poem being dedicated to him.

Towards the end of February 1950, Ginsberg was released and went back to Paterson to live with his father and stepmother. His uncle Leo landed him a job as a reporter on the *Labor Herald,* and he tried to impose a structured routine to his life. It was during this stay in Paterson that Ginsberg first wrote to New Jersey's most famous literary son, William Carlos Williams. Williams was a poet in the tradition of Whitman, an artist who brought to life the vernacular rhythms of the American voice – "word of mouth language, not classical English," as he himself put it. "No ideas but in things" was his imagist dictum, and one he put into practice with poems as diverse as "The Red Wheelbarrow" and "Paterson." "I inscribe this missive somewhat in the style of those courteous sages of yore who recognized one another across the generations as brotherly children of the muses," wrote Ginsberg somewhat grandly to Carlos Williams, enclosing nine of his poems. Carlos Williams was delighted by the letter, though less so by the poetry. He found it too vague and ornate, too self-consciously poetic. Yet an important correspondence had begun, and Carlos Williams was to be one of the towering figures in Ginsberg's career.

Meanwhile Ginsberg's new-found heterosexuality was also finding an outlet through an older woman by the name of Helen Parker. Ginsberg became a convert, rejecting his "queerness" as "morbid" and "unnecessary," and embracing the straight-world with an evangelical zeal. There was talk of them moving in together, and, despite sceptical letters from Burroughs, the rest of his friends were convinced that he was genuinely happy and settled. When he and Helen split up, Ginsberg embarked on a spree of heterosexual flings.

His work-life was also fluctuating, moving from

In September 1951, Burroughs shot his wife, Joan Vollmer, while playing a drunken "William Tell" game. (© Fred W. McDarrah.)

journalism to market research and back to unemployment. With nothing better to do, he took a trip to visit Burroughs who by now had moved to Mexico City.

Meanwhile, Joan Vollmer's mental state had deteriorated even further, her drinking and Benzedrine-use having taken on a reckless, even suicidal, quality. On September 6, 1951, she and Burroughs had spent the day drinking and trying to sell a handgun. In a moment of drunken abandon, Burroughs said, "It's about time for our William Tell act," even though it was the first time they had ever played it. Joan placed a glass on her head and Burroughs fired one shot from a .38 automatic. The glass fell to the ground, undamaged. The pronouncement of Joan's death at the Red Cross Hospital was a pure formality – she was dead before she hit the ground. Ginsberg learned of the accident in the evening paper, and in a letter to Neal Cassady reflected that his imagination was "too limited to comprehend the vast misery and absurdity and sense of dream that must exist in Bill's mind now."

Like the Kammerer–Carr case, Burroughs's accidental shooting of Joan exposed the dark side of the Beat's *laissez-faire* lifestyle. Years later Ginsberg would write of dreaming about Joan and asking her, "What knowledge have the dead?" In the immediate aftermath, however, he reacted with stunned incomprehension.

Chapter

4

Previous page: Ginsberg
immediately sensed a soul-
mate when he met Peter
Orlovsky in 1954.
(© Corbis.)

By 1951 Ginsberg's circle of friends
included Alan Ansen.
(© Allen Ginsberg Trust.)

Ginsberg's new apartment was at 346 West
15th St., and it was here that he composed
many of the poems that ended up in *Empty
Mirror*. Cassady and Kerouac had moved to
San Francisco, but Ginsberg had no shortage
of friends. His circle included Carr, the writer
John Hollander, Alan Ansen, a young
outlaw poet called Gregory Corso and Carl Solomon who had begun working as an editor
for his uncle (A.A. Wyn) at Ace Books. This is the first incarnation of Ginsberg as
switchboard – approaching Ace as an agent first for Kerouac and then for Burroughs's
*Junky*. Wyn published the latter in 1953, but it would be six years before Kerouac's book
found a home.

    In encouraging others, Ginsberg seemed to motivate himself. He began to
concentrate on Carlos William's poetics, chopping out the
ornamental but inert material, so that he was left with
word sketches. These he would arrange according to
breath, syllable-stress and rhythm. He nervously sent

Ginsberg composed many
of his *Empty Mirror* poems
at his apartment on 346
West 15th St.
(© Bill Morgan.)

them to Carlos Williams whose response was ecstatic: "Wonderful!" he wrote back, "You *must* have a book. I shall see that you get it. Don't throw anything away. These are *it*."

Carlos Williams's enthusiasm was not matched by the publishing world, and Ginsberg suffered a string of rejections. It would be the best part of a decade before *Empty Mirror* was published.

Burroughs arrived back in New York in August 1953. His friendship with Ginsberg took on an intensity of passion that seemed to have surprised both of them. Ginsberg was able to hold his own more intellectually, as well as having the sexual advantage of youth. Burroughs was increasing the pressure on the younger man, talking about how their identities could melt into one ("schlupping," he called it) and trying to persuade Ginsberg to follow him to Tangier. They would talk late into the night, every night. Ginsberg recalled that he was flattered that his mentor should want him so badly – "I thought he was my teacher, so I'll do what I could to amuse him . . . I kinda felt privileged" – yet at the same time, he felt smothered by Burroughs's demands, eventually telling him, "I don't want your old cock." Burroughs was wounded and Ginsberg full of

New York poet outlaw Gregory Corso was introduced to the Beats in 1951. (© Allen Ginsberg Trust.)

**Ginsberg visited Mexico in 1954 and became entranced by the Mayan ruins. (© Allen Ginsberg Trust.)**

regret. In December Burroughs shipped out to Tangier.

Ginsberg headed first for Florida then on to Mexico, where he became entranced by the Mayan ruins and a female archaeologist. To his friends, Ginsberg appeared to have gone missing; their letters to him were returned unopened, while he was unaware that his were also going astray. Burroughs waited to hear from him like an addict: "I did not think I was hooked on him like this," he wrote to Kerouac, "the withdrawal symptoms are worse than the Marker habit. One letter would fix me." He got his hit by May 24: "Thank God he is O.K. I don't know what I would do without him." Yet Ginsberg was still feeling cautious towards him, and was already bound for San Francisco, where things were not much quieter.

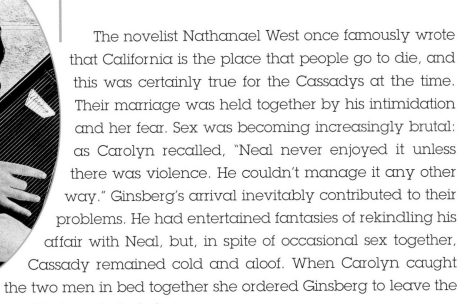

In 1954 Ginsberg met the luminaries of San Francisco's bay area, including poet and playwright Michael McClure. (© Larry Keenan, Jr.)

The novelist Nathanael West once famously wrote that California is the place that people go to die, and this was certainly true for the Cassadys at the time. Their marriage was held together by his intimidation and her fear. Sex was becoming increasingly brutal: as Carolyn recalled, "Neal never enjoyed it unless there was violence. He couldn't manage it any other way." Ginsberg's arrival inevitably contributed to their problems. He had entertained fantasies of rekindling his affair with Neal, but, in spite of occasional sex together, Cassady remained cold and aloof. When Carolyn caught the two men in bed together she ordered Ginsberg to leave the house, and personally drove Ginsberg to Berkeley.

Armed with a letter of introduction from William Carlos Williams, he set about meeting the luminaries of San Francisco's bay area. Kenneth Rexroth, Michael McClure, and Robert Duncan all became friends, while a

Kenneth Rexroth was M.C. at the seminal event where Ginsberg first performed "Howl." (© Gene Anthony.)

65

A performance of Robert Duncan's *Faust Foutu* at a Fillmore Street art gallery generated the idea of holding poetry readings there. (© Fred W. McDarrah.)

woman called Sheila Boucher quickly became his lover. Much to Burroughs's horror, Sheila and Ginsberg moved in together, driving another nail in the coffin of Burroughs's romantic hopes. "I think I'm responsible for single-handedly destroying Bill's belief in love," Ginsberg would later reflect. Yet they continued to correspond, and several of Burroughs's letters to him would occur as routines in his novel *Naked Lunch*.

Ginsberg eventually told Sheila of his homosexual history, particularly his relationship with Cassady. She was horrified, and their relationship began to deteriorate. One night, following an argument, Ginsberg stormed out and wandered into "Polk Gulch," a bohemian area centred around Foster's Cafeteria and the Hotel Wentley. He met the painter Robert La Vigne who invited him back to his home, and there he encountered a canvas portrait of Peter Orlovsky – a large oil painting of the twenty-one-year-old Russian–American who had recently been discharged from the army and had enrolled in classes at San Francisco City College. As if on cue, Orlovsky walked into the room and was a

A party and outdoor reading on Telegraph Hill, San Francisco. Events of this kind were becoming popular by the mid-1950s. (© Jerry Stoll.)

vision equal to that of his portrait. Ginsberg immediately sensed a soul-mate and they spent a night together of sexless cuddling, Ginsberg writing to Kerouac soon after about the wonders of this perfect boy. He had to return to New York for his brother's wedding, but when he arrived back Ginsberg moved into La Vigne's with Orlovsky, as La Vigne was soon to leave for San Diego.

After his experiences with Cassady and Burroughs, Ginsberg trod cautiously in his courtship of Orlovsky. His journals of the time are racked with a mixture of self-doubt and overwhelming passion. "I wonder what Peter feels," runs one entry, "I don't

Fugazi Hall in North Beach was the venue for many poetry and performance events. (© Jerry Stoll.)

Soon after meeting Peter Orlovsky, Ginsberg wrote to Kerouac about the wonders of his "perfect boy." (© Fred W. McDarrah.)

know, he never expresses it, though there is a lot of sex and affection in his body. I don't know how to act . . . Cannot ask him yet, too early, though I am afraid of hearing something less moving than what I feel . . . Wish for a moment between us when I could weep unguardedly the relief. Can't yet, he won't like me that way now." Another entry asks, "Does he know I'm trying to do this? Is he interested if I am? And if he is not, how to have strength to give and not be tormented continually by cravings until I turn masochistic and mad and abuse myself before him & be rejected?"

In February 1955, any doubts were removed when they make a pledge: "We made a vow to each other that he could own me," Ginsberg recalled, "my mind and everything I knew, and my body, and I could own him, and all he knew, and his body; and that we would give each other

This page: Painter Robert La Vigne first introduced Ginsberg to Orlovsky, and they later stayed together in his apartment.
(© Larry Keenan, Jr.)
Overleaf: Ginsberg and Orlovsky, 1955.
(© Allen Ginsberg Trust.)

ourselves, so that we possessed each other as property, to do everything we wanted to, sexually or intellectually, and in a sense explore each other until we reached the mystical 'X' together, emerging two merged souls."

It is ironic that having been scared off by Burroughs's "schlupping" suggestion, he should initiate a similar pact himself. Yet, despite Orlovsky's professed heterosexuality, it was a vow that would last more than thirty years.

Although he had initially encouraged it, La Vigne became jealous of their relationship and Ginsberg left to take his own apartment on Montgomery St., Orlovsky going with him.

"Married" life sat well with Ginsberg; he and Orlovsky bought a car and took brief vacations. He was receiving $30 a week unemployment and emersing himself in his writing. He enrolled at Berkeley to study for his Masters in English, and while waiting for term to start began writing a poem that would change his life beyond all recognition.

The front room of the Montgomery St. apartment where Ginsberg wrote "Howl." (© Allen Ginsberg Trust.)

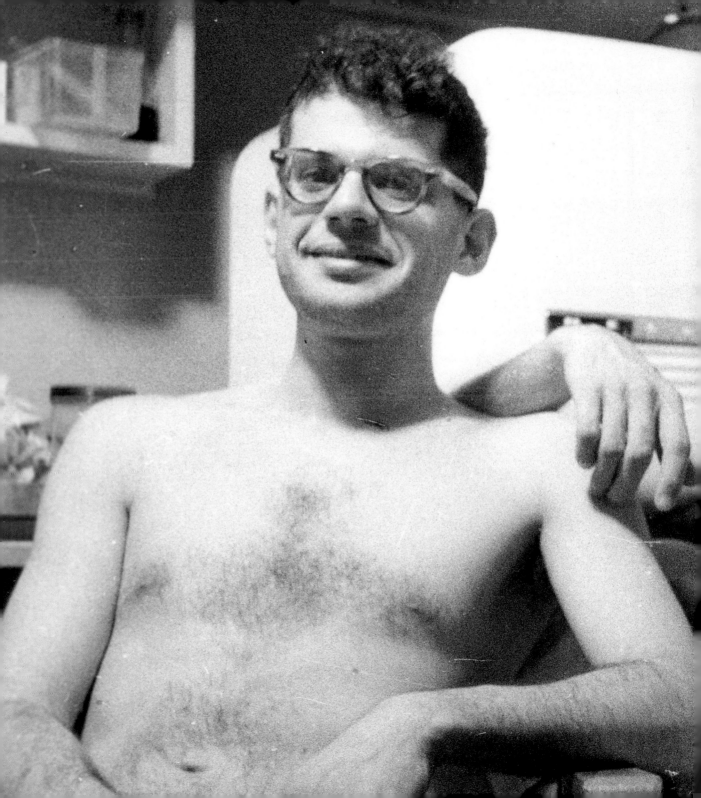

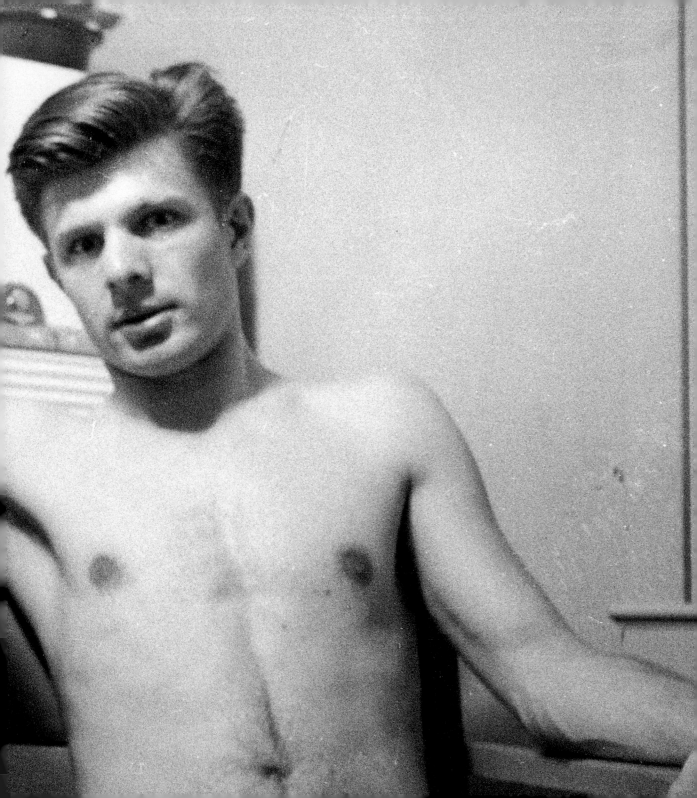

Chapter

5

Previous page: Ginsberg outside
the hotel where he envisioned
"Moloch" in "Howl."
(© Harry Red.)

Ginsberg began writing "Howl" in August 1955, intent on conjuring up what he described as "a tragic custard-pie comedy of wild phrasing . . . like Charlie Chaplin's walk, long saxophone-line chorus lines." His method took its cue from Kerouac's emphasis on spontaneity – what he called the "undisturbed flow from the mind of personal secret idea-words, blowing (as per jazz musician) on subject of image." The first section of the poem tumbled out of him over a couple of days. It was an incantation – a defiant celebration of the madman who had been destroyed by corporate America. Among its lists and cumulative rhythms could be heard the democratic spirit of Walt Whitman and the street-slang cadence of Carlos Williams.

Yet it was in performance that the poem's full potential would be realized. Robert Duncan had staged his play *Faust Foutu* at a renovated garage-art gallery on Fillimore St., and its success had generated the idea of holding a poetry reading there. Michael McClure was originally asked to organize it, but passed on the responsibility to Ginsberg. Rexroth was recruited as the M.C., and the programme consisted of Philip Lamantia, Michael McClure, Gary Snyder, Philip Whalen and Allen Ginsberg.

The evening of October 13, 1955 has

Ginsberg began writing
"Howl" in August 1955.
(© Allen Ginsberg Trust.)

entered into Beat legend. In his book *The Dharma Bums*, Kerouac relayed the event: "Scores of people stood around in the darkened gallery straining to hear every world of the amazing poetry reading as I wandered from group to group, facing them and facing away from the stage, urging them to glug a slug from the jug, or wandered back and sat on the right side of the stage giving out little wows and yesses of approval and even whole sentences of comment with nobody's invitation but in the general gaiety nobody's disapproval either."

In a piece entitled "West Coast Rhythms," *The New York Times* expressed astonishment at this "freewheeling celebration of poetry . . . The audience participates, shouting and stamping, interrupting and applauding. Poetry here has become a tangible social force, moving and unifying its auditors." Ginsberg read the first section of "Howl," and the atmosphere became electric. At the end of each line a drunken Kerouac shouted "Go" – a refrain

Philip Lamantia performed alongside Ginsberg in the event held in October 1955 that changed the course of Beat history. (© Fred W. McDarrah.)

Ginsberg was introduced to
Gary Snyder by Rexroth in 1955.
(© Allen Ginsberg Trust.)

that was taken up by the rest of the audience. As Michael McClure later wrote: "Ginsberg read on to the end of the poem, which left us standing in wonder, or cheering and wondering, but knowing at the deepest level that a barrier had been broken, that a human voice and body had been hurled against the harsh wall of America and its supporting armies and navies and academies and institutions and ownership systems and power-support bases."

Present at the reading had been Lawrence Ferlinghetti, co-founder of the City Lights Bookstore. On his return home he sent Ginsberg a telegram: "I greet you at the beginning of a great career. When do I get the manuscript?"

Over the next few months Ginsberg busied himself completing sections two and three of "Howl," as well as re-working section one. Despite his allegiance to spontaneity, the final version of the poem was arrived at after nineteen drafts. His studies at Berkeley petered out, and he turned for his education to his fellow poets. As he later wrote, "A word on the Academies: poetry has been attacked by an ignorant and frightened bunch of bores who don't understand how it's made, and the trouble with these creeps is that they wouldn't know poetry if it came up and buggered them in broad daylight."

From Snyder and Philip Whalen he received instruction in Buddhism and backpacking, while he remained in regular correspondence with Carlos Williams. Rexroth remained a pivotal figure – a kind of Beat patrol around which most of San Francisco's renaissance revolved. Another poetry reading was organized at Berkeley, although this time the performances were recorded. Poetry had spilled over into theatre, their readings evoking the deranged spectacle of Artaud a generation before.

Ginsberg settled into his new house – on Milvia St. – and applied to the Military Sea Transportation Service, hoping the pay would fund a trip to Europe. He began sending proofs of "Howl" to America's literati, most notably Eliot, Pound, Trilling, Van Doren and Faulkner. Carlos Williams naturally received one, opening it to find in introduction the famous battle-cry: "Hold back the edges of your gowns. Ladies, we are going through hell."

By May 1956 Ginsberg had begun

It was by Snyder and Philip Whalen that Ginsberg was introduced to Buddhism and backpacking.
(© Larry Keenan, Jr.)

In 1955 Ginsberg and Orlovsky
pledged commitment to one
another and began to enjoy
"married" life.
(© Allen Ginsberg Trust.)

his training as a Military Sea Serviceman. He moved his belongings to Orlovsky's apartment and sublet his Milvia St. cottage to Philip Whalen. A month later he received a telegram telling him that his mother had died. She had been ill for some time; in fact his journal entries before her death record anxiety dreams in which she had already died. His entry that night read:

Death of Naomi June 9, 1956 –
Tenderness & a tomb – the world is a tomb of tenderness
Life is a short flicker of love.
When out into the grass knelt down & cried a little – to heaven for her. Otherwise nothing.

Lawrence Ferlinghetti, co-founder of
City Lights Books, attended
Ginsberg's reading of "Howl" and
immediately sent him a telegram
requesting a copy of the manuscipt.
(© Larry Keenan, Jr.)

Yet the journals are otherwise sparse in recording his responses. It would be in his epic poem "Kaddish," that Ginsberg finally did his mourning.

Taking with him the proofs of "Howl," Ginsberg set sail for Alaska. He returned in September and was eager to begin his travels. His plan was to hitchhike to Los Angeles, move on to Mexico City, return to New York, join Burroughs in Tangier, and then onwards into Europe.

He arrived in L.A. in October and, along with Corso, gave a reading to an audience that included Anaïs Nin. A drunken heckler asked what they were trying to prove. "Nakedness," replied Ginsberg and took off all his clothes. "The way he did it was so violent and direct," wrote Nin, "it had so much meaning in terms of all our fears of unveiling ourselves."

In Mexico he and Orlovsky hooked up with Kerouac, who shared the car journey to New York with them. Ginsberg's stay there was a blizzard of activity. He visited his mother's grave, met Salvador Dali, was introduced to Orlovsky's family and met the poet

Previous page: (left to right) Bob
Donlan, Neal Cassady, Ginsberg,
Robert La Vigne, and Lawrence
Ferlinghetti outside City Lights
Books, 1955.
(© Allen Ginsberg Trust.)

Diane Di Prima. He took Kerouac, Corso and Orlovsky to meet Carlos Williams. When asked by Kerouac for some words of wisdom, the seventy-three-year-old poet responded, "There's a lot of bastards out there." Ginsberg visited Carl Solomon in Pilgrim State Hospital and wrote the visit up as verse.

He made the rounds of virtually every publisher in New York, touting not just his own

work but also that of Snyder, Whalen, Robert Duncan, McClure, and Robert Creeley. "I went on this big push and went all over everywhere I could," he recalled. "I went on a campaign to introduce all this new poetry to unwilling editors." Even on the cusp of his own success, Ginsberg was tireless in promoting his contemporaries.

Orlovsky and Ginsberg arrived in Tangier on March 22 – a visit which was to put a strain on their relationship. Burroughs was jealous and suspicious of Orlovsky – "Peter and Bill didn't get along," recalled Ginsberg. "Bill rejected Peter quite a bit,

Ginsberg's puja (prayer) table.
(© Lisa Law.)

In Mexico Ginsberg met Salvador Dali
and was introduced to Peter's family.
(Standing) Kerouac, Ginsberg, Orlovsky.
(Kneeling) Corso, Lacfadio Orlovsky.
(© Allen Ginsberg Trust.)

'cause he saw him as a rival. Although Peter and I tried to take Bill to bed – figured we'd give him all he could get, exhaust him."

The main focus of activity, however, was Burroughs's *Naked Lunch*, with Ginsberg spending six hours a day typing up and editing the manuscript. By May they had more than two hundred pages.

The next month saw them bound for Europe. They went first to Spain, stopping off at Granada, Seville, Madrid and Barcelona, then on to Venice to stay with Alan Ansen. Ginsberg was much taken with Italy, soaking up its art galleries and monasteries, paying homage to the graves of Shelley and Keats. He slept outside the church of St. Francis, arguing with the monks about original sin. He was entertained by Mary McCarthy and Nicholas Calas, and inadvertently offended the majestic Peggy Guggenheim. He met W.H. Auden and spent a drunken night arguing with him about Walt Whitman. It had been an idyllic summer, and as it drew to a close he and Orlovsky prepared to move to Paris.

While Ginsberg was exploring the culture of Europe, his poetry was under threat from

Overleaf: Ginsberg and Orlovsky
made a trip to Tangier in 1957.
(Left to right) Orlovsky, Kerouac,
Burroughs.
(© Allen Ginsberg Trust.)

Ginsberg constantly touted the work of others, including Robert Creeley, as well as his own. (© Jonathan Williams.)

his native America. On May 21 two police officers went to City Lights Bookstore and bought a copy of "Howl." Two warrants were obtained, and Lawrence Ferlinghetti was arrested along with the clerk who had sold them the book. A date of August 22 was set for the trial. The American Civil Liberties Union offered themselves as defense and the bay area's literary community prepared to do battle. "The literary backup was impeccable," said Ginsberg. "You couldn't possibly lose the case, so I didn't take it seriously as a threat." And yet it was a cause célèbre in San Francisco. Nine expert witnesses testified on the poem's behalf, and a flood of critical support arrived from editors, academics, booksellers and poets. Rexroth, Robert Duncan, Kenneth Patchen, and James Laughlin were just a few of the voices who insisted on being heard. According to Ferlinghetti's notes on the trial, the prosecution put forward two "expert" witnesses – one a private elocution teacher, and the other from the Catholic

University of San Francisco. Their cross-examinations now read like parodies of their profession. Having heard the evidence, Judge Clayton Horn concluded on October 3:

"I do not believe that 'Howl' is without even 'the slightest redeeming social importance.' The first part of 'Howl' presents a picture of a nightmare world; the second part is an indictment of those elements in modern society destructive of the best qualities of human nature; such elements are predominantly identified as materialism, conformity and mechanization leading toward war. The third part presents a picture of an individual who is a specific representation of what the author conceives as a general condition . . . It ends in a plea for holy living . . .

"In considering material claimed to be obscene it is well to remember the motto: 'Honi soit qui mal y pense [Evil to him who thinks evil].'"

In the words of Ferlinghetti, "Thus ended one of the most irresponsible and callous police actions to be perpetrated west of the Rockies, not counting the treatment accorded Indians and Japanese." Ginsberg could not have asked for better P.R. By the end of the trial his book had more than 10,000 copies.

August 22, 1957 was the date set for the "Howl" trial. Shown here (front row) are Lawrence Ferlinghetti and "Shig" Murao, the clerk at City Lights Books who sold the arresting officers the book.
(© Allen Ginsberg Trust.)

Chapter

6

Previous page: In 1961 Ginsberg and Orlovsky travelled to India, a trip funded by the royalties from "Howl."
(© Allen Ginsberg Trust.)
This page: On rue St.-André-des Arts, Paris.
(© Corbis.)

In moving to Paris, Ginsberg and Orlovsky were joining a tradition of literary exile – an American lineage that stretched from Gertrude Stein and Alex B. Toklas to Richard Wright and James Baldwin. 9 rue Git-le-Coeur would enter into legend as the Beat hotel, a place populated by jazz musicians, hookers and painters, "a fleabag shrine where passers-by move out of the way for the rats," according to one journalist. Corso had been persuaded to join them on his way to Germany, and one journal entry simply states: "Peter needs a shave. I need a bath. Gregory needs a new personality." An illness of his brother's forced Orlovsky to return to New York, and his place was taken by a newly arrived Burroughs. The set-up now had echoes of their old 115th St. apartment. The sexual unease that had plagued Ginsberg's and Burroughs's relationship was replaced by a platonic bonding. The older man voiced his intentions to undergo psycho-analysis, and Ginsberg told Orlovsky, "He no longer needs me like he used to, doesn't think of me as a permanent future intimate sex schlupp lover," adding later, "Now I see Bill is really on same connection and I begin to feel connected with everything and everyone."

In London, Thomas Parkinson, Ginsberg's advisor at Berkeley, was producing a series of poetry readings for the B.B.C. and invited his ex-student to contribute. "Enchanted in England/weeping at the foggy earth of England's Blake," was how Ginsberg poeticized it. He ended up recording the whole of "Howl" and "A Supermarket in California," telling Orlovsky he "gave slow sorrowful reading, built up, almost broke down in tears again, dreaming I was talking thru microphone to the Soul in the Fog, read to Blake himself." During his three-week stay, he visited the British Museum, Stonehenge, Salisbury Cathedral and Oxford University where he gave an impromptu reading. It was in England that the first notes for his poem "Europe! Europe!" were composed.

Ginsberg would return briefly to England in May, but otherwise remained in Paris until his departure in July. He was introduced to Man Ray and the dadaist Tristan Tzara. He met (and kissed) Duchamp, and took Burroughs to visit Celine where they exchanged prison stories and compared

Corso in his attic room at 9 rue-Git-le-Coer – the "Beat Hotel." (© Allen Ginsberg Trust.)

drug anecdotes. He spent a drunken night with Henri Michaux, and is reputed to have peed in his sink. Yet Ginsberg felt intellectually isolated in Paris: "Nothing was happening poetically, and they were very conservative, and very proud of themselves, because they have this great literary tradition in France and everything (including my own style) came from France. And they had had this big deal with Existentialism, which was Sartre and Camus, but it was more rationalistic and novelistic and very little poetry – there was no grand lyricism."

"Last Poem There" is his final entry in Paris, a description of his room and how it is inhabited by memory:

The first petty miracle of
contemplation, sign from
the body
Look in the mind and
eat the monster there.

The next day he headed back to New York.

Kerouac and Ginsberg:
"Know-Nothing
Bohemians," according to
Norman Podhoretz.
(© John Cohen.)

Ginsberg and Orlovsky
rented an apartment on
170 East 2nd St.
(© Bill Morgan.)

Ginsberg returned to an America that was dancing to a mixed Beat – successful publishing phenomenon on the one hand, a cause for moral censure on the other. Ironically Norman Podhoretz led the attack. Although he had earlier bemoaned the lack of spirituality amongst the intellectuals of his own class, he then did a volte-face in an essay on "The Know-Nothing Bohemians." "The spirit of the Beat Generation," he wrote with all the indignity he could muster, "strikes me as the same spirit which animates the young savages in leather jackets who have been running amok in the last few years with their switchblades and zip guns." His prose reaches apoplexy in its conclusion that, "There is a suppressed cry in [the Beats'] book: Kill the intellectuals who can talk coherently, kill the people who can sit still for five minutes at a time, kill those incomprehensible characters who are capable of getting seriously involved with a woman, a job, a cause."

He was not alone. The magazine *Playboy*, fuelled partly by a sense of rivalry, ran a three-part special on "The Beat Mystique." Its argument was that the Beats lacked ambition, were "modern-day nihilists for whom it was enough, apparently, to flout and

It was in the East 2nd Street apartment that Ginsberg wrote his elegy "Kaddish." (© Fred W. McDarrah.)

deny." Their sexual license *Playboy* did not deny, but insisted that it was a cover-up for their frigidity: "When the hipster makes it with a girl, he avoids admitting that he likes her. He keeps cool. He asks her to do the work, and his ambition is to think about nothing, zero, strictly from nadaville, while she plays bouncy-bouncy on him."

Not wanting to be left behind, *Life* magazine ran a vitriolic satire on "The Only Rebellion Around" which caricatured the Beat with his "sandals, chinos, and turtle-necked sweater and studying a record by the late saxophonist Charlie Parker." They were, *Life* assured its readers, the "sick little

The Beat poets began to receive letters from girls asking them to come and "cool us in." (© Fred W. McDarrah.)

bums" who "emerge in every generation". And yet the vehemence with which the Beats were attacked served only to prove their visibility. Kerouac's work was selling impressive amounts; City Lights had published Corso; LeRoi Jones began publishing *Yugen* which contained work by Ginsberg, Creeley, Charles Olson, and Frank O'Hara; Holmes wrote "The Philosophy of the Beat Generation" for *Esquire* magazine; and Beat poets were receiving letters from girls in Kansas telling them that their town was "Squaresville itself" and asking them to come and "cool us in." In demonizing the Beats, Podhoretz and *Playboy* helped generate their allure.

It was to this climate of radical discontent that Ginsberg returned. He and Orlovsky rented an apartment on 170 East 2nd St., paid for by Orlovsky's job at the same psychiatric hospital to which his lover had been admitted so many years ago. Ginsberg continued to promote his contemporaries, urging Ferlinghetti to publish Whalen, Snyder,

Dick Seaver of Grove Press (left) and Irving Rosenthal of *Big Table*, the magazine set up in response to pressure to stop publishing Beat writing. (© Fred W. McDarrah.)

and Burroughs, as well as dedicating himself to his own verse. It was at this point that the bulk of "Kaddish" was written – an exhausting forty-hour explosion of writing in which he evoked the line-breaths of mournful tribute.

In the guise of Beat agent he went to Chicago where Irving Rosenthal and Paul Carroll had published Beat writing in their university magazine *Chicago Review*. Both men were under pressure from the authorities to drop pieces by Kerouac and Burroughs from their next issue. Their response was to resign and set up their own magazine, *Big Table*. Corso and Ginsberg gave readings to raise money for the new venture, and in so doing came even more under the media spotlight. *Time* magazine devoted a page to them, while for the *Chicago Sun–Times* they were front-page news. When Ginsberg read at the Sherman Hotel he pulled a crowd of more than 800 people.

This number would be doubled when he returned to Columbia to read at McMillin. Among the crowd was Diana Trilling who gave a positive, if somewhat patronizing, account of the evening in her article "The Other Night at Columbia." A flavor of Trilling's prose can be tasted via the parody that Robert Bly wrote of her piece: "My name is Diana Trilling and I am very important. My husband is Lionel Trilling and he is also very important. Between the two of us, we are so important that everything we do, think, or say deserves a lot of space in the *Partisan Review* . . .

"It is a shame that Ginsberg didn't turn out to be more like Lionel, when he had such a perfect model!" he goes on. But then again so did Trilling:

"I took one look at the crowd and was certain that it would smell bad. Columbia students are all so dirty. Nevertheless, they smelled all right. The audience was clean and Ginsberg was clean and Corso was clean and Orlovsky was clean, and the kitchen was clean and the politics were clean and we are all good clean Americans."

It is a testament to the impact of the Beats that not only were they reviewed, but that those reviews themselves were deemed worthy of satire.

The readings took on a momentum of their

Corso, Ginsberg (back), Paul Carrol, and Orlovsky following a reading in Chicago to raise money for *Big Table*.
(© Allen Ginsberg Trust.)

own. The poets performed at Harvard, Brooklyn College, and the Gaslight Cafe and George Washington University, D.C. Berkeley asked Ginsberg back to read, which he did to an audience that included the poet Stephen Spender.

After a gruelling tour of the East Coast and extensive work on anthologies, magazines (*Beatitude* in particular) and manuscripts, Ginsberg accepted an invitation to a literary conference in Chile to be held in January 1960.

"Ginsberg was liked both as an artist and as a melancholy, black-bearded Boy Scout in exile," reported the *San Francisco Chronicle* on his conference performance:

"He talked in Spanish, made numerous speeches, danced and asked questions." Yet the most significant aspect of the visit was his introduction to the drug Ayahuasca, a mind-expanding hallucinogen that he experienced as a religious experience. "A revolution in the Hallucination," was how he

Ginsberg's interest in psychedelics led to his involvement in Timothy Leary's psilocybin experiments at Harvard. (Left to right) Ginsberg, Mrs. Leary, Timothy Leary, and Lawrence Ferlinghetti.
(© Allen Ginsberg Trust.)

described it to Burroughs. "Still feeling like a Great lost Serpent-seraph vomiting in consciousness of the Transfiguration to come – with the Radiotelepathy sense of a Being whose presence I had not yet fully sensed . . . the more you saturate yourself with Ayahuasca the deeper you go – visit the moon, see the dead, see God." Ginsberg's correspondence with Burroughs on the effects of the drug comprised the second part of their book, *The Yage Letters*. So impressed was he with his new find, that on his return to New York he brought large quantities of the drug back with him.

His interest in psychedelics led him to Harvard University where Dr. Timothy Leary was conducting experiments with psilocybin – the psycho-active ingredient of magic mushrooms. After his first trip Ginsberg became a convert, suggesting a list of people who might act as the drug's advocate. Willem de Kooning, Theolonious Monk and Robert Lowell were among the volunteers. So too was Kerouac, but as Leary wrote in his book *Flashbacks*, he "remained unmovably the Catholic carouser, an old-style Bohemian without a hippie bone in his body. Jack Kerouac opened the neural doors to the future, looked ahead, and didn't see his place in it."

This clash between the King of the Beats and the Guru of the Hippies suggests the disparity between their projects. The flower-children may have wanted to lay claim to

Kerouac, but he grew to despise what he saw as their un-American outlook. Indeed, as Barry Miles's biography of him points out, Kerouac was a right-wing Republican with anti-Semitic leanings. He supported Joe McCarthy, defended the Vietnam War and, in the more extreme throes of alcoholic oblivion, would burn crosses on his lawn in support of the Klan. It is a measure of Ginsberg's altruism that he remained loyal to their friendship. Yet, at the same time, the Leary connection may have been the point at which Ginsberg's focus of

**Ginsberg and Orlovsky reunited with Burroughs in Tangier in 1961. (Left to right) Orlovsky, Burroughs, Ginsberg, Alan Ansen, Paul Bowles (seated), Corso, and Ian Sommerville. (© Allen Ginsberg Trust.)**

Burroughs pretending to hang Ansen. By this time Burroughs had entered a dark time in his life, believing that people were aliens and language a virus. (© Allen Ginsberg Trust.)

aesthetic and political interest began to shift. Certainly he would embrace the Utopianism of the sixties with the same passionate curiosity with which he had defied the conformity of the fifties.

Ginsberg and Orlovsky returned to Paris in April of 1961 hoping to find Burroughs. At this point, however, Burroughs had entered his psycho-years, believing that people were aliens, women should be eradicated, his friends were all agents and language was a virus. He had moved back to Tangier and it was here that the pair caught up with him. Burroughs mercilessly ridiculed Orlovsky, launching mean-spirited attacks on his heterosexuality and lack of reading. Burroughs's behavior was indeed intended to alienate and, after a week of goading, Orlovsky had had enough and left for Greece. It would be the first time in seven years that he would break their wedding vow.

When Burroughs moved to London, Ginsberg was left alone in Tangier, broke, rejected and alienated. With no particular plan or direction, he went first for Greece then on to Tel Aviv where he re-united with Orlovsky. Their next stop would be India and a long overdue reunion with Gary Snyder.

With the royalties from "Howl" and a favorable rate of exchange, Ginsberg and Orlovsky could afford to explore Indian culture in all its diversity. They travelled from Bombay to Deli, there hooking up with Snyder and his then wife, Joanne Kyger. They took in the Himalayas and the Ganges, rode the Pathankat Express, explored the Ajanta and Ellora caves. They met the Dalai Lama who introduced them to new forms of meditation. They mingled with Indian poets, were interviewed by the local newspapers, and soaked up the opium dens and red-light areas where the eunuchs were the star attraction. Looking back on these months, Ginsberg credited India with helping him to become less cerebral, to focus on the physical rather than the metaphysical dimension of his being: "A whole series of Indian holy men pointed back to the body – getting *in* the body rather than getting out of the human form. But living in and inhabiting the human form." It had taken fifteen years, but it was here in India that he was finally able to relinquish his Blake

At the foothills of the Himalayas with Gary Snyder (left), with whom Ginsberg and Orlovsky had an overdue reunion in 1962.
(© Allen Ginsberg Trust.)

In British Columbia in 1963, Ginsberg taught alongside Robert Creeley (right, with his wife, Bobbie) and Philip Whalen. (© Allen Ginsberg Trust.)

vision, a shift that would later be celebrated in his poem "The Change."

At a reading at the Hindu university in Benares, where they lived for five months, Ginsberg and Orlovsky were brought to the attention of the local C.I.D., the audience having been outraged by the poet's apparent profanity. The C.I.D. put them under almost constant surveillance, bursting into their rooms, demanding to see their papers and going through their poetry. At one point they were even told to leave the country, and it took a visit to the head of the Home Ministry before the harassment ceased.

The combination of police scrutiny and Orlovsky's increasing drug dependency was making Ginsberg feel agitated. It was with no small sigh of relief that he accepted Robert Creeley's invitation to teach poetry at Vancouver University for three weeks in the summer.

After brief sojourns in Cambodia and Tokyo, Ginsberg arrived in British Columbia in July of 1963 where he taught alongside Olson, Robert Duncan, Denise Levertov and Philip Whalen as well as Creeley. It was during this spell that he began to blend music into his readings, accompanying himself with an Indian harmonium and singing as a form of poetic delivery.

This was the beginning of Ginsberg the shaman – his straggling hair and Old Testament beard adding to his mystical promise. The Beat-rebel was transforming himself into a witch-doctor of the word, a man who was combining the alchemy of art with a politics of spirituality. The rogue student was fast becoming an "in-vogue" teacher.

Chapter 7

Previous page: In the Glacier
Peak Wilderness Area,
Washington State, 1965.
(© Allen Ginsberg Trust.)

The sixties are a decade that come steeped in clichés, as though history itself is a barrage of newspaper headlines: the assassination of Kennedy, civil rights sit-ins, Ho Chi Minh chanting, black power salutes, hippie love-ins, draft-card burnings, riots in Chicago, killings on campuses, streets on fire. Yet the discontent that crystallized the decade can be seen to have its origins in the fifties. The murder of Emmett Till in 1955 precipitated a wave of black outrage – a feeling that would find its most concrete incarnation when Rosa Parks refused to relinquish her bus seat to a white man. The image of the Panther may belong to the sixties, but its genesis can be located ten years earlier. As the historians Alexander Bloom and Winni Breines have persuasively argued, "These decades, then, are more complex, more ambiguous, and more interconnected than popular imagery suggests. The events and perspectives of the sixties did not spring full blown and brand new into American life. For the 1960s, the 1950s are past as prologue."

This sense of continuity can be found in the ease with

At the Vancouver Poetry Conference, 1963. (Clockwise from top left) Jerry Heiserman, "Red," Ginsberg, Bobbie Creeley, Warren Tallman, Robert Creeley, Charles Olson, Don Allen, Philip Whalen, and Thomas Jackrell.
(© Allen Ginsberg Trust.)

which Ginsberg moved from the Beat rebellion to the politics of the counter-culture. His involvement in the anti-war movement and black civil rights can be seen as an extension of his "Howl" of protest and his celebration of the "negro streets." "We are people of this generation," began the founding statement of the Students for a Democratic society, "bred in at least modest comfort, housed now in universities, looking uncomfortably to the world we inherit." The language of affluence and education are here juxtaposed with that of discomfort, a tension which suggests how the children of the sixties had also been the adolescents of the fifties.

One such figure was a folk-singer by the name of Bob Dylan – a hobo-troubador who arrived in New York in 1961 on the trail of Woody Guthrie. As he told his biographer, Clinton Heylin, "I didn't start writing poetry until I was out of high school. I was eighteen or so when I discovered Ginsberg, Gary Snyder, Philip Whalen, Frank O'Hara and those guys."

After Dylan's first two albums, Ginsberg had begun to reciprocate the interest. He heard in Dylan a kindred spirit, an artist who combined the energy of protest with the mystical magic of what he was to call his "chains of flashing images."

By December 1963, Ginsberg had returned to New York and was staying with the

Ginsberg began to campaign
tirelessly for the legalisation of
marijuana. Here he leads a demonstration in Hyde Park, London.
(© Topham.)

publisher Ted Wilentz. Through a mutual friend, the journalist Al
Aronowitz, the two poets met and struck up an instant rapport. It
was a friendship that would last throughout Ginsberg's lifetime,
involving creative collaboration. Most famously Ginsberg
appeared in Dylan's video for "Subterranean Homesick Blues" in
the film *Don't Look Back*, but would also provide the sleeve notes
to the album Desire, and write three poems in the early seventies
in praise of the singer's work. For his part, Dylan would write, "why
allen ginsberg was not chosen to read poetry at the inauguration
boggles my mind," on the sleeve of "Bringing it All Back Home."

The cross-fertilization between Ginsberg and Dylan is yet
another example of how he combined a deeply personal vision
with a sense of being involved in a more collective project. Indeed,
the whole period 1963–64 saw an even more pronounced
involvement with the politics of the artistic community. Ginsberg
testified in defence of Jack Smith's underground film *Flaming
Creatures*, and, along with Norman Mailer, would give a spirited

critique of *Naked Lunch* when it was tried for obscenity. He campaigned tirelessly for the legalisation of marijuana, holding demonstrations and speaking out for the drug in the *Herald Tribune*. He edited Huncke's writing, published one of Burroughs's routines and made a cameo appearance in one of Warhol's "Couch" films. If Dylan was beginning to provide the soundtrack for the counter-culture, Ginsberg gave it both a face and the networks which were essential in sustaining its momentum.

Despite his left-wing sympathies, Ginsberg's politics maintained a peculiarly American streak – as *laissez-faire* libertarianism that was as committed to freedom of sexuality and expression as it was to providing economic critiques of capitalism. When he was invited to a writer's conference in Cuba in early 1965, he was shocked to find a "socialist utopia" that was hostile to "bourgeois deviations" such as homosexuality and experimental art. The focus of the revolution had been literacy, hospitals and schools, and displayed scant tolerance towards Ginsberg's revolution of the head.

On his arrival in Havana, Ginsberg immediately found himself caught up in the contradictions of post-revolutionary Cuba. He was interviewed by national magazines and newspapers, and, although he

Michael McClure, Bob Dylan and Ginsberg. In Dylan, Ginsberg heard a kindred spirit, and the two struck an instant rapport.
(© Larry Keenan, Jr.)

expressed sympathy for Castro's treatment by America, he consistently spoke out against Cuba's use of the death penalty and their persecution of homosexuals.

Cuba's population was no more than six million, a figure that meant that the arrival of this American subversive could not easily be ignored. Rumor and gossip became speculation and fact, and Ginsberg seriously aroused the suspicion of the authorities. He met the Minister for Culture, unwittingly insulting her with ironic comments and over-familiarity. Poets and journalists he had befriended began to be arrested; a scheduled reading at the city's university was inexplicably cancelled. When the rest of the delegates were invited to meet the Prime Minister, Ginsberg was conspicuously passed over. As one journal entry read: "Total collapse today – woke totally isolated, didn't know who to talk to, to confide in . . . Entering Orwellian dream-world – Total suppression of conscious and unconscious fantasy everywhere . . . Can't trust anyone. Like having a nervous breakdown."

Yet Ginsberg persisted, giving informal lectures on Whitman and Carlos Williams, and attempting to apologize to the affronted Culture Minister. It was all to no avail. In the early hours of a February morning, Ginsberg was woken by three revolutionary militiamen who took him to the chief of immigration. He had upset too many people on

Ginsberg travelled to
Moscow in 1965, where he
arranged to meet Joe
Levy, his mother's cousin.
(© Allen Ginsberg Trust.)

too many issues. The next day he was escorted on to a plane bound for Czechoslovakia.

Ginsberg's artistic network proved as reliable as ever, with him contacting Josef Skvorecky on his arrival in Prague. The Czech writer took the American to his heart, introducing him to the underground clubs and alternative cafés where Ginsberg was already a cult name.

With his royalty checks and performance fees he could afford a trip to Moscow, where he was made a guest of the Writers Union. This trip was a homecoming of sorts, his maternal grandparents having come from Lvov. Within days he had arranged to meet Joe Levy, his mother's cousin, leading to an emotional reunion; Ginsberg had been five the last time they had met, which had been in Newark. He absorbed Moscow with the hunger of a tourist, taking in the Kremlin, Saint Basil's Cathedral, the Pushkin, and the museums of Dostoevsky and Mayakovsky.

He arrived back in Prague just before May Day. The recently revived custom of this holiday was for the people to hold an election and crown the King of May. Skvorecky had originally been selected to stand, but had declined at the last minute owing to illness. Ginsberg gleefully took his place and, in Staromestske Square, in front of a crowd of 100,000, Ginsberg was elected the King of May 1965. When the Secretary for Cultural Affairs discovered what had happened, he insisted that the ruling be overturned. Although Ginsberg's reign had been short-lived, he compensated by drinking and singing with his entourage throughout the night.

The damage, however, had been done. Some notebooks of his had already come to the attention of the authorities, and his May crown had been the final straw. Over the next four days he was twice pulled over by the police and once assaulted by a complete stranger. Two more police interrogations followed in which it was affirmed that his writing

was against the interests of the state, and that his sexual behavior posed a threat to the country's youth. On May 7 Ginsberg was escorted to yet another airport, deported from yet another country.

Ginsberg's political excursions to Cuba and Eastern Europe are, in many ways, the mirror-

In front of a crowd of 100,000, Ginsberg was crowned Prague's King of May, 1965.
(© Allen Ginsberg Trust.)

image of American foreign policy, the need to find new frontiers (expansion being the nation's Manifest Destiny) ironically echoing the poet's attempt to extend his own psychic frontier. Cuba's sexual politics may not have been the most liberal, but Ginsberg's refusal to accept another culture's "morality" testifies to his own peculiarly American sense of his inalienable rights (and rightness).

Ginsberg's next stop was London, a city that had not yet officially started to swing, but was certainly on the verge of doing so. Dylan was touring there – the raw material that would end up in Pennebaker's "Don't Look Back" – and Ginsberg hooked up with him at the Savoy. In "Days in the Life," a collection of voices from the English underground recall their first meeting with Ginsberg. Barry Miles – the "Clark Kent of the Underground"

– was the prime mover in introducing Beat writing into English culture: "I was managing the paperback section of Better Books. En route to New York from Prague, Ginsberg stopped off in London. Having got to London he came in to Better Books. He had nowhere to stay. We immediately suggested that he did a reading there. So Ginsy came in and I offered to put him up

During his stay in London in 1965, Ginsberg performed a reading at the Royal Albert Hall, an event organized by Barbara Rubin.
(© John Hopkins.)

Ginsberg, McClure, and Connor chanting at Ginsberg's San Francisco home, 1965. (© Larry Keenan, Jr.)

and he moved in with us in Hanson Street. He gave a reading at Better Books which, even though we didn't advertise it, was totally packed."

David Widgery, the left-wing activist and counter-cultural thinker, had a more colorful encounter: "I went to interview Allen Ginsberg for *Sixth Form Opinion*. When he was in London for the poetry reading I attached myself to him, not knowing anything about sex in general and homosexuality in particular, and Ginsberg took a tremendous fancy to me and seduced me. I eventually managed to escape on my Lambretta and got home with a sore bum and a bit of apprehension."

It was on his birthday that the poet had his legendary encounter with the The Beatles. Miles again: "He didn't know them but he wanted to know them and was introduced to them by Dylan. It wasn't a very successful meeting. Then in '65 on his birthday, June 3, he wanted to have the Beatles to his birthday, he thought that would be nice . . . George and John came to the birthday party, which was held in Chester Square. The trouble was

Ginsberg had a cameo role
in one of Andy Warhol's
"Couch" films.
(© Kate Simon.)

that by the time John and George arrived, with their wives, Allen had taken all his clothes off and had his underpants on his head and a No Waiting sign hanging round his dick. John was very upset at finding Allen completely naked . . . [he] told me, 'You don't do that in front of the birds.'"

If London was enamored of Ginsberg, he was equally enchanted by the city's energy. Poets and radicals seemed to be everywhere, and it was this sense of possibility that led Barbara Rubin to hire the Albert Hall for a poetry reading. Accounts differ as to the evening's success. Certainly Ginsberg was drunk and disappointed at his own performance; although other participants such as Spike Hawkins were "totally astounded by it." Johnny Byrne, the Liverpudlian Beat, experienced it as both: "It was like a fantasy that they'd had of how things should be and how things should go and suddenly they'd woken up and it was really happening. And that sense of unreality carried all the way

The Last Gathering of Beat
Poets and Artists, City
Lights Books, 1965.
(© Larry Keenan, Jr.)

through the entire proceedings. There were those at the heart of it who saw it as the great opening up and believed that it would lead on to bigger and better poetry recitals and the coming together of people. I sensed immediately that, ironically, it was actually the last of the poetry readings . . . It had to be savored then, because it was not going to be around tomorrow."

Michael Horovitz, another of the evening's poets, makes the point that, "The Albert Hall brought a lot of things that were happening together and reduced the uptightness and competitiveness and intellectual distancings and refinements and narcicissim and vanity . . . And these little local feuds were put into perspective, because all over the world there were other people in similar situations; that changed things and it became more international."

The counter-culture was no longer confined to a series of scenes: a larger drama was in play.

Ginsberg had not only achieved fame, he had also had it thrust upon him. His photograph stared out from mainstream as well as underground magazines, whilst he became a regular fixture on television and radio. His was the voice that could be relied upon to give a good quote, an embodiment of sexual, political and artistic dissidence. His profile was as recognizable as Che Geuvara's, his speeches as impassioned as those of Malcolm X. "Don't follow leaders/Watch your parking meters," sang Dylan. And everyone smiled as they spotted Ginsberg in the background.

Having explored Europe, Ginsberg returned to re-acquaint himself with America. His first stop was New York where he found a dilapidated apartment in Alphabet City; then on to California to attend the Berkeley Poetry conference.

Berkeley and Oakland were just some of the places that were echoing to the chant of "Hey, Hey, L.B.J., How Many Kids Did You Kill today?" Before a crowd of 25,000 in front of the Washington Monument, Paul Potter threw out the challenge to "The people of this country to end the war in Vietnam, and to change the institutions which create it . . . The people of this country must create a new social movement – and if that can be built around the issue of Vietnam then that is what we must do."

Berkeley was taking him at his word, organizing a march in October that resulted in a pitch-battle with the Hell's Angels. Despite being America's self-styled outlaws, the Angels' politics were pitched somewhere between the John Birch Society and the K.K.K. They may have been romanticized by the counter-culture, but they themselves had little time for what they considered to be Beatnik communism. When another demonstration was organized for November, Ginsberg acted as go-between between the protesters and the Angels.

Shortly before the planned march, Ginsberg wrote a letter-poem to the Angels that was published in the *Berkeley Barb*. In it he pointed to a "mutual sympathy," and argued that,

If you attack, & having innocent pacifists, youths & old ladies busted up

AND CRITICIZED AS IRRESPONSIBLE COWARDS
By you, by Press, by Public and by Violence loving leftists
& rightists . . .

then the Angels would be playing into the hands of "the heat." Incredibly,

In 1966 Ginsberg became involved with the Leary Defense Fund and Congressional hearings on L.S.D. (© Allen Ginsberg Trust.)

Ginsberg's diplomacy payed off, and the Angels instead wrote to Lyndon B. Johnson:

"Dear Mr President:

On behalf of myself and my associates I volunteer a group of loyal Americans for behind the lines duty in Vietnam. We feel that a crack group of trained gorrillas [*sic*] would demoralize the Viet Cong and advance the cause of freedom. We are available for training and duty immediately."

The Angels saved face, the march went ahead and L.B.J. never got around to replying.

According to Hunter S. Thompson, "The outlaws had never encountered anyone quite like Ginsberg; they considered him other-worldly. 'That goddam Ginsberg is gonna fuck us all up,' said Terry. 'For a guy that ain't straight at all, he's about the straightest sonofabitch I've ever seen. Man, you shoulda been there when he told Sonny he loved him . . . Sonny didn't know what the hell to say.'"

Early in 1966 Ginsberg and Orlovsky once again took to the road. They returned first to Big Sur – the setting of Kerouac's autobiographical novel – then on to the Santa Monica mountains where they met Christopher Isherwood. Next to Albuquerque to see Robert Creeley, followed by Kansas where Ginsberg gave readings, interviews and was filmed by Robert Frank giving one of his performances. His nomadic travels, with their litany of hotels and stop-offs, recall the drifting of Nabokov's Humbert – an America that combined a landscape of leisure with an undercurrent of danger. Of course it was Vietnam not Lolita that was the focus of Ginsberg's obsession, and it was during this period that he composed "Wichita Vortex Sutra" – a poem that challenged America with the same mystical curse that his "Howl" had thrown down a decade earlier.

During this time, Ginsberg was effectively rootless, dividing his time between New York and L.A., involving himself with Warhol, the Leary Defense Fund and congressional hearings on L.S.D. On January 19, 1967 he took part, along with Snyder and Leary, in the most famous "happening" of the hippie era. San Francisco's Golden Gate Park played host to the "Human Be-In" – a coming together of the politics of Berkeley University and the drug-driven quests of Haight-Ashbury. Helen Swick Perry recalled a "world [that] was new and clean and pastoral. Children wandered around in the nude. People sat on the grass with nothing to do, sometimes moving up near to the small platform where a poetry reading might be going on, or where a band might be playing." Later on in the afternoon she recalls, "A man attached to a billowy parachute that looked like a huge cloud drifted down from the sky above; no one announced it but the message seemed to go soundlessly throughout that huge crowd of tens of thousands of people; and we all looked up into the sky with a single ripple of turned heads and eyes. No airplane was heard, there was no sign of where he came from, and we all treated it as a latter-day miracle."

As the poet Larry Fagin told Miles, "Allen really became the Allen that we know in 1967. He got out into the public and could never really withdraw completely again. The Be-In Skyrocketed the whole Ginsberg cottage industry into outer space. It was the highest visibility that he had had up to that point."

Given his profile, it was inevitable that Ginsberg would come under authority-scrutiny. Friends of his were being busted with alarming regularity and, after a reading at his hometown in Paterson, a warrant was issued for his own arrest. It was with some relief that Ginsberg accepted an invitation from the British Arts Council to attend an international poetry festival in the summer of 1967.

Ginsberg's arrival in London coincided with a party attended by Marianne Faithful, Mick Jagger and a selection of hash cookies. The Stone's singer invited the poet to accompany his band on a song they had written about a previous drugs arrest. The song was "We Love You," an ironic tribute to a country whose drug policy even *The Times* admitted to being like breaking butterflies upon a wheel.

**Overleaf: On January 19, 1967 Ginsberg took part in the "Human Be-In" in Golden Gate Park, San Francisco. (© Lisa Law.)**

Ginsberg spent a month in Milan befriending the eighty-one-year-old Ezra Pound (left).
(© Allen Ginsberg Trust.)

An alternative conference was also due to take place at that time in London. R.D. Laing had called for a "Dialectics of Liberation" – a meeting of minds that could weld his own maverick brand of anti-psychiatry with the more direct concerns of political activism.

The contributors included the black activist Stokely Carmichael, Emmett Grogan, Julian Beck (of Living Theatre fame), Michael X and Ginsberg. According to Sue Mills, the event was pivotal but acrimonious: "The Dialectics were very important, extraordinary. That was Kingsley Hall – Joe Berk, Ronnie Laing and all those people – and they were really very, very clever people . . . I went with Ginsberg. It was quite frightening. Stokely Carmichael started this tirade against whitey. Though one could see perfectly well why he had that point of view, it was completely unworkable. Then there was this meeting back at the house where he [Ginsberg] was staying and there was extreme bad feeling and a huge argument and split between them all. Allen was going, 'This is dreadful. We have not argued this long for everyone to start getting at each other's throats and getting divided. This is not going to get us anywhere.'"

Clearly hippiedom's universal consciousness had little time for racial diversity, and the in-fighting that plagued the counter-culture can arguably be seen as the white middle-classes' refusal to challenge their own assumptions.

The next stop was Milan where he spent a month befriending the eighty-one-year-old Ezra Pound. The Great Modernist had by this time retreated into virtual silence, although most eye-witnesses maintain that the old man appreciated the younger one's company and attention. "Make It New" had been Modernism's dictum, and, if they had nothing else in common, Ginsberg had certainly responded to its aesthetic challenge.

Chapter

8

Previous page: Ginsberg reading at
San Francisco State College, 1967.
(© Gene Anthony.)

Returning to New York in November 1967, Ginsberg and Orlovsky attempted to settle back into their old routine. Orlovsky was drug-free and Ginsberg's reputation afforded them entry into any of the hip circles of their choice. The first of these was a meeting with the Maharishi – a spiritual leader who had achieved notoriety through his association with The Beatles. The two gurus displayed a mutual respect, though clashed over their stances on drug use and Vietnam. It is another testament to Ginsberg's mixture of open-mindedness and irony that he swapped ideas with the Maharishi without either dismissing or being converted to them. Again, the figure of Ginsberg the prophet is

In 1968 Abbie Hoffman enlisted Ginsberg's support for the Yippie Festival of Life. The event became a battleground, Ginsberg's mantra's answered with tyrannical state force. (© Fred. W. McDarrah.)

juxtaposed with that of the political pragmatist.

Perhaps more suited to Ginsberg's taste was the Youth International Party – the Yippies – founded by Jerry Rubin and Abbie Hoffman. Early in 1968, Hoffman visited Ginsberg in the hope of enlisting his support. Their plan was to organize a Festival of Life in which they would run a pig for President. Ginsberg agreed to take part. In the "Yippie Manifesto," Hoffman wrote: "On election day let's pay tribute to rioters, anarchists, Commies, runaways, draft dodgers, acid freaks, snipers, beatniks, deserters, Chinese spies. Let's exorcise all politicians, generals, publishers, businessmen, Popes, American Legion, A.M.A., F.B.I., narcos, informers.

"And then on Inauguration Day Jan. 20 we will bring our revolutionary theatre to Washington to inaugurate Pigasus, our pig, the only honest candidate, and turn the White House into a crash pad. They will have to put Nixon's hand on the bible in a glass cage."

By 1967, Ginsberg had achieved the highest point of visibility he had had so far, and would never completely withdraw from the public eye again. Here shown at the Artists Liberation Front Meeting, San Francisco. (© Lisa Law.)

The festival was due to take place in Lincoln Park, and to coincide with the Democratic Convention of Chicago. Mayor Daley drafted in more than 11,000 police, 5,000 national guards, and 7,000 state troops. The battle-lines had been drawn. Burroughs, Jean Genet and Ginsberg were all present, but the most enduring account of the three-day battle surely belongs to Norman Mailer. In his book *Miami and the Siege of Chicago* he wrote: "Monday night, the city was washed with the air of battle. Out at the stockyards, some hours after the convention had begun, the streets were empty but for patrol cars and police barricades at every approach . . . The Chicagoan hiding this Monday night (as he was to hide Tuesday night, Wednesday night, Thursday night) inside his home was waiting perhaps for an eruption of the Blacks or an avalanche of Yippies to storm the chastity of his family redoubts. So fear was in these empty streets, and the anger of the city at its own fear, an anger which gave promise not soon to be satisfied by measures less than tyranny . . .

"It was after eleven," Mailer continued, "even close to midnight, and police cars were

Along with Abbie Hoffman, Jerry Rubin, co-founder of the Youth International Party, was put on trial for conspiracy to incite a riot following the Festival of Life. (© Fred W. McDarrah.)

Ginsberg became increasingly involved in taking on the challenge to end the war and change the institutions that created it.
(© Larry Keenan, Jr.)

everywhere, and platoons of policemen every few hundred feet, enough for a parade . . . In the dark there was no way to count, perhaps a few thousand in all of the park, youths up for an event with every muted mix of emotions, fear as clean as skiers before a steep downhill run, and vigorous crazy gaiety in the air like college pranksters before a pantry raid; with it, the night nonetheless not without horror, very much not without horror, as if a fearful auto accident had taken place but ten minutes before and people wandered about now in the dark with awareness that bodies wrapped in bloodstained blankets might be somewhere off a shoulder of the road."

Just as the Human Be-In of the previous year had been supplanted by a full-scale riot, the

The Yippies wanted to "inaugurate Pigasus, our pig, the only honest candidate, and turn the White House into a crash pad." (© Fred W. McDarrah.)

park in Chicago became a battlefield where Ginsberg's mantras were answered with tyrannical state force. The merciless police assault was turning Utopian visions into a brutal dystopia. Mailer again: "Ginsberg had been tear-gassed, his throat so injured he could hardly speak – and since the chanting of his Hindu hymns was a spiritual manna for Ginsberg, how the injury to his voice would hurt. And worse. Seventeen newsmen had been attacked by police, a photographer for the *Washington Post*, two reporters for the *Chicago American*, one for the *Chicago Daily News*, two photographers and a reporter for the *Chicago Sun-Times*, a reporter and a photographer for Life, cameramen for three television networks, and three reporters and a photographer for *Newsweek* magazine . . .

"The counter-revolution had begun. It was as if the police had declared that the newspapers no longer represented the true feelings of the people. The true feelings of the people, said the policemen's clubs, were with the police."

As the protesters counted their casualties, and the streets of Chicago were still smouldering, a recently elected governor of California named Ronald Reagan announced that, "Experience has shown that prompt dealing with disturbances leads to peace, that hesitation, vacillation and appeasement lead to greater disorder." He went on to ask his audience, "From which group will we . . . elect your leaders? Will it be from the few, but militant, anarchists and others now trying to run our campuses? Or will we elect our future leaders from the majority of fine young men and women dedicated to justice, order and the full development of the true individual?"

The battle of Chicago was far from over. In December 1969 a trial was held accusing David Dellinger, Rennie Davis, Abbie Hoffman, Jerry Rubin, Tom Hayden, Lee Weiner, John Froines and Bobby Seale with conspiracy to incite a riot. So outspoken was Seale (a freedom that one would have thought was defended by the first amendment) that he was gagged and bound to his chair throughout the proceedings. If ever there was a metaphor for the silencing of the African–American this was surely it, and yet the jury still managed to find him guilty.

Ginsberg was called to testify, and, to the baffled amusement of the court, repeated the chanting he had sung at the convention.

**After the Chicago Democratic Convention: Burroughs, Terry Southern, Ginsberg, and Jean Genet. (© Michael Cooper.)**

Cherry Valley Farm, Upstate New York, which became Ginsberg's retreat from the struggles elsewhere. (© Jonas Kover.)

According to Hayden: "The conflict of identity on this level was sharpest during Ginsberg's testimony . . . The conflict came out into the open during Foran's cross-examination. Instead of questioning Allen about anything he had testified to – such as pre-convention planning by the Yippies and permit negotiations – Foran asked him to recite and explain three sexual poems apparently selected by the Justice Department agent at the table, a young, bespectacled, high-voiced, short-haired, blue-eyed young man named Cubbage. The first was about a wet dream, the second about a self-conscious young man at a party who discovers that he is eating an asshole sandwich, the third about a fantasy of sleeping between a man and a woman on their wedding night. At Foran's request, Allen recited each one calmly and seriously and then tried to answer the prosecutor's sarcastic query about their religious significance . . . When Allen left the stand we were in tears. Court recessed a few minutes later, and Foran

Herbert Huncke joined Ginsberg and Orlovsky in 1968 to assemble more of his writings. (© Allen Ginsberg Trust.)

138

stared at Allen and said, 'Damn Fag.'"

As a respite from the urban struggles in Illinois, Ginsberg headed back east with Orlovsky. He had bought a farm in Upstate New York – a ninety-acre retreat five miles outside Cherry Valley. Huncke had gone with them and was assembling more writings, having already had his journal published.

Here Ginsberg extended his interest in music, purchasing a second-hand pump organ which could accompany his singing of Blake's poetry. In the midst of the anti-war movement, the rural life provided much-needed relief. The group, Barbara Rubin among them, were effectively self-contained. They grew their own food, repaired their property, and tried to immerse themselves in conversation and contemplation. They kept

Barbara Rubin was among the self-contained group living at Ginsberg's farm and gathering their resources.
(© Fred W. McDarrah.)

animals, installed a fish-pond and appeared to be the epitome of Emersonian self-reliance.

While the group were re-gathering their resources, Kerouac's had continued to fall apart. By 1968 his alcohol-dependency was full-blown. He spent his days slumped in front of his mother's TV set drinking beers and whiskey-chasers. In the middle of the night he would ring up his friends and savagely berate them in his drunken oblivion. On October 21, 1969 his cirrhotic liver finally exploded, drowning the writer in his own

The farm became a haven for the literati who were burned out from the city. (Left to right) Ginsberg, Orlovsky, Denise Mercedes, Bonnie and Ray Bremser, Julius Orlovsky, Alan Deloach, Gregory Corso. (© Gordon Ball.)

blood. The following day Ginsberg and Orlovsky paid tribute to him at a reading at Yale. They chanted the Diamond Sutra, going on to recite stanzas from Kerouac's "Mexico City Blues." Their friendship had been stormy, often abusive, and it was only Ginsberg's tolerance that had sustained it. As late as 1985 Ginsberg was still persuading the Lowell Preservation Commission to honor one of its most famous sons. He gave readings to raise money, and in June 1988 a $100,000 granite monument was erected in Eastern Canal Park. The Jack Kerouac Commemorative is a testament not only to the writer, but also to the tireless commitment and industrious efforts of his most long-suffering of friends.

The farm became a haven for the literati who were burned out by the city. Having got back into speed, Orlovsky kicked the drug during his time there, sweating and hallucinating while Ginsberg nursed him back to health. The writers Bonnie and Ray Bremser were frequent visitors, as were the poets Robert Creeley and John Giorno. Carl Solomon paid a visit in an attempt to soothe his nerves. Gergory Corso came to stay,

Bonnie and Ray Bremser were frequent visitors, as was poet John Giorno (opposite). (© Fred W. McDarrah.)

only to cause conflict with his constant baiting of Orlovsky and his irritation at the farm's relative sobriety.

This movement between the city and the country, the political and the pastoral, once again shows Ginsberg's ability to hover between worlds. In taking to his farm he did not turn his back on the anti-war movement; by the same token, his involvement with the trial of the Chicago Eight in 1969 did not preclude him exploring his own version of the American idyll. His talent was in bringing together disparate cultures, welding together ideologies that appeared to be at odds. Committed to urban and rustic alike, he continued to remain engaged with the importance of engagement itself.

Chapter

9

Previous page: Ginsberg,
Gary Snyder and others.
(© Gene Anthony.)

By the end of the decade, the idealism of "the movement" had begun to turn sour in the mouths of its members. Assassinations were almost seen as government policy, and the rhetoric responded in kind. As Eldridge Cleaver said, "The assassin's bullet not only killed Dr. King, it killed a period of history. It killed a hope, and it killed a dream . . . [It was] a final repudiation by white America of any hope of reconciliation, of any hope of change by peaceful and nonviolent means. So that it becomes clear that the only way . . . is to meet fire with fire."

The Weathermen took him at his word – going underground and advocating guerrilla warfare. As one of their pamphlets argued, "What's new is that today not quite so many people are confused, and a lot more people are angry; angry about the fact that the promises we have heard since first grade are all jive; angry that, when you get down to it, this system is nothing but the total economic and military putdown of the oppressed peoples of this world . . .

"But the lies are catching up to America – and the slick rich people and their agents in government bureaucracies, the courts, the schools, and the pig stations just can't cut it anymore."

The bullet was beginning to seem more viable than the Buddha, and history was

On May 4, 1970, the National Guard opened fire on students at Kent State University, Ohio. (© Topham.)

appearing to demonstrate this. On May 4, 1970, the National guard opened fire on the students of Kent State University, Ohio. Four people were killed, nine more were injured. The tactics of Vietnam were being reproduced on the streets of America. Ten days later, similar gunshots rung out at Jackson State College. One of the guardsmen was recorded on tape as saying, "There's two nigger females and three males we just discovered, that's a total of ten . . . Here's another one, let me see what this is." The statistics vary, but all persons killed or wounded by gunshot were black.

The Woodstock festival of August 1969 may have held out a promise of communal love, but it was soon superceded by the events at Altamont. A free concert organized by the Stones soon descended into mayhem when a young black man, Meredith Hunter, was kicked and beaten to death directly in front of the stage by a bunch of drug-crazed

Previous page: The Woodstock
festival of August 1969 may have
held out a promise of communal
love, but it was soon superceded by
the events of Altamont.
(© Baron Wolman.)

Ginsberg struck a deal with
Trungpa Rinpoche whereby
Ginsberg became the poetic guru
and Trungpa the spiritual one.
(© Allen Ginsberg Trust.)

Angels. Rock 'n' roll was becoming more equated with death than with peace – a shift that would continue with the deaths of Janis Joplin, Jim Morrison and the butchery of that thwarted rock-star Charles Manson. In an article for *Liberation* magazine, Julius Lester summed up the tasks that lay ahead with as much resignation as optimism: "We had the dream and we are losing it . . . Before we can create the revolution which will make real the dream, we must begin to create it amongst ourselves. In the beginning it was easy to maintain the dream. Now, because the problems facing us are more complex than we imagined, maintaining the dream is that much more difficult. Letting that dream suffuse our every thought, word and deed is that much more difficult. Yet, that is what we must do, no matter how difficult it becomes."

One response to such difficulties would be for Ginsberg to adopt Chögyam Trungpa as a mentor – a Tibetan Buddhist whose "wild wisdom" had more in common with the earlier Beats than with the present-day political radicals. He encouraged Ginsberg to shave off his beard and improvize during readings. It was through him that Ginsberg took the formal vows of Buddhism at the Dharmadhatu centre for meditation and accepted the title "Lion of Dharma." Trungpa asked him to be his poetry mentor, and a deal was struck whereby Ginsberg became the poetic guru and Trungpa the spiritual one. Their relationship led to Ginsberg taking his meditation more seriously, learning new mantras and disciplining himself to a daily routine. His new techniques would later be celebrated in his collection "Mind Breaths."

His involvement with the anti-war movement was constantly at odds with the violence that was often involved. The demonstrations in Miami of 1972 resulted in pitch-battles between the Vietnam Vets and the police; Ginsberg had hoped for "a peaceful festival of life," but instead spent three days in jail on a charge of disturbing the peace. He saw the Vets as sabotaging the movement, although there is substantial evidence that it was the F.B.I. who were sabotaging the Vets. Individual campaigns seemed more suited to his position, and he fought and wrote tirelessly for the release of Leary who had been imprisoned for possession and Hoffman who had been arrested for dealing.

Yet Trungpa was the man with whom he felt

Ginsberg had hoped that the 1972 Miami Democratic Convention would be a "peaceful festival of life," but instead he spent three days in jail. (© Ray Fisher.)

151

most at ease. In 1973 he accepted an offer to spend three months teaching at a Buddhist seminary in Teton Village, Wyoming. Religion spilled over into art, and Trungpa's Naropa Institute at Boulder invited him to read poetry there. It was here, along with Anne Waldman, that he established the "Jack Kerouac School of Disembodied Poetics" – a school that survives to this day.

With the exception of his campaigns, Ginsberg spent most of the early seventies alternating between meditation and poetry readings. He would spend up to nine hours a day concentrating on his breathing – attempting to rid himself of his worldly ego. This would be balanced against performances in which he would read "Ego Confession", a poem that proclaimed, "I want to be known as the most brilliant man in America." This balancing act suggests a figure pitched somewhere between Pynchon and Mailer – a writer who, on the one hand, yearns for the freedom of anonymity, and on the other is one huge advertisement for himself – again, a quintessentially American movement.

Late in 1973 Ginsberg visited Burroughs in London. He found his friend drunk and lethargic, his complexion as gray as the English weather. On his return to New York he persuaded City College to hire

Trungpa's Naropa Institute at Boulder invited Ginsberg to read poetry there. (Left to right) Robert Duncan, Anne Waldman, Trungpa Rinpoche. (© Allen Ginsberg Trust.)

Burroughs to teach on their newly formed creative writing programme, and in February 1974, Burroughs returned to New York.

A year later a benefit reading took place at Columbia as a fund-raiser for the Naropa Institute. It was a re-enactment of the infamous event of 1959, with Orlovsky, Corso and Ginsberg all reading alongside Burroughs. It was the first time the group had been reunited in public for more than fifteen years. In re-visiting his old university, Ginsberg displayed just how far he had moved – from being an oddity to an elder statesman. What had once been the shock of the new now had the ring of the nostalgic. He read from "Wichita Vortex Sutra," "Wales Visitation," and "Please Master." Along with Burroughs he received rapturous applause and the kind of adulation usually reserved for rock-stars. Columbia's outcast had returned like the Prodigal Son.

By 1975 Ginsberg and Orlovsky had moved to an apartment on East 12th St., a spacious affair that allowed them separate rooms as well as an office in which to work. Later that year Bob Dylan embarked on a tour he called the Rolling Thunder Revue. It was to be a concept tour, a mixture of theatre and music which would also be filmed. Joan Baez had come on board, as had Ramblin' Jack Elliott, Bob Neuwirth, and Sam Shepard. *Rolling Stone* magazine describe it as, "Bob Dylan's travelling band of gypsies, hoboes,

**Brion Gysin and Burroughs. Ginsberg visited Burroughs in London in 1973, finding his friend drunk, lethargic and gray.**
**( Charles Gatewood.)**

lonesome guitar strangers and spiritual green berets . . . The tour buses would roll out from the Gramercy Park Hotel, where the Revue had been holed up, and head up to Plymouth, Massachusetts, for the first stop of a whirlwind blitz of the Northeast, running from four to six weeks."

Dylan asked Ginsberg to join them, and, as Mel Howard recalled, "Allen saw Dylan rightly connected to the whole tradition of the Beat generation and through that to the earlier poets, Poe, the whole sense of the American vagabond. So Allen was keen to add that element." Their intention was to play small clubs, venues of no more than 3,000 capacity. It was to be a travelling circus with the cameras rolling, a film that would end up as *Renaldo and Clara*. On the first night Ginsberg joined in a rendition of "This Land is Your Land," and throughout the tour made appearances either as a harmonist or a poet. Shepard was originally hired to script the movie, although it soon developed a life of its own. Dylan: "There was a lot of chaos while we were making the film. A lot of good scenes didn't happen because we had already finished improvising them by the time the cameras were ready to film. You can't recapture stuff like that. There was a lot of conflict during filming. We had people who didn't understand what we were doing because we didn't have a script. Some who didn't understand were willing to go along with us anyway."

Ginsberg clearly fell into the latter camp, and two of the film's most memorable moments involve Ginsberg explaining the Stations of the Cross to Dylan at a Catholic grotto in Lowell, and the two men paying a visit to Kerouac's grave. Again Mel Howard noted, "There were all these themes running through it. Ginsberg had the idea of Dylan as an alchemist, rediscovering America," and Ginsberg himself wrote, "And behind it all the vast lone space of No God, or God, mindful conscious compassion, lifetime awareness, we're here in America at last, redeemed. O Generation, keep on working!"

In his "Rolling Thunder Logbook" Shepard recounts the trope rehearsing in a resort hotel in Massachusetts in front of an audience of retired Jewish ladies: "The mothers go from patient acquiescence to giggled embarrassment to downright disgust as Allen keeps rolling away at them (he was reciting "Kaddish") . . . There's something in the air here that I can't quite touch, but it feels close to being volcanic. Something of generations, of mothers, of being Jewish, of being raised Jewish, of Kaddish, of prayer, of America even, of poets and language."

The off-stage scenes of the movie may now seem lame with self-indulgence – the triad of Dylan, his wife Sara and Joan Baez is more like an encounter group than an emotional drama – yet the performances still resonate, Dylan's white-faced top-hatted presence a captivating mixture of troubador, minstrel and clown. As Ginsberg describes it on the sleeve-notes to *Desire,* "thin Chaplinesque body dancing to syllables sustained by Rolling Thunder band rhythm following Dylan's spontaneous ritards & talk-like mouthings for clarity . . . Big discovery, these songs are the culmination of Poetry-music as dreamt of in the '50s & early '60s – poets reciting-chanting with instruments and bongos – Steady rhythm behind the elastic language, poet alone at microphone reciting-singing surreal-history love text ending in giant 'YEAH!.'"

His father's ailing health forced Ginsberg to take time out from the Rolling Thunder

In April 1975 Corso, Burroughs, Ginsberg, and Orlovsky read at Columbia, a re-enactment of the event held there in 1959. (© Fred W. McDarrah.)

Tour. Louis was now in his eighties and was virtually housebound. He was suffering from pancreatic cancer as well as spots on the lungs, a condition from which there was no hope of cure. "Louis is dying in Paterson," wrote Ginsberg to Corso, "wasted thin arms, wrinkled breasts, big belly, skull nose speckled feet thin legs." On July 8, 1976 Louis died peacefully in his sleep. Returning on a plane to bury his father, Ginsberg composed the poem "Father Death Blues." In his last interview for the B.B.C., he cited the poem as one through which he would most like to be remembered. The program concluded with him singing it, the poem almost becoming his own requiem:

> Hey Father Death, I'm flying home
> Hey poor man, you're all alone
> Hey old daddy, I know where I'm going.

"I think it's the fruition of my Buddhist training," he observed. Trungpa had said, "I extend my thought to your father and the people of the sky. Please let him go and continue your celebration."

After the tour and his father's death, Ginsberg became embroiled in a dispute back at Colorado. The poet W.S. Merwin had had a bitter experience with Trungpa at the Eldorado Lodge in Snowmass, Colorado. Though technically not a Naropa event, it was one that would nonetheless reflect badly on the whole institution. It began with disputes over Buddhist theology, with Merwin often refusing to join in the obligatory chanting. However, things came to a head during a Halloween party in 1975, when Trungpa arrived at the party drunk, and "persuaded" several female guests to strip naked before doing so himself. (Trungpa's championing of the spiritual benefits of alcohol was in fact disguising a long-standing

In 1975 Ginsberg joined Bob Dylan on his Rolling Thunder Revue tour, a mixture of theatre and music which was also filmed.
(© Fred W. McDarrah.)

drink problem.) He then summoned Merwin and the poet Dana Naome to join in, but they pointedly refused. The more insistent Trungpa's assistants became, the more adamant were the poets in their refusal. Crowds began to gather to witness this battle of wills, and a mini-riot ensued with Merwin throwing broken bottles and Naome screaming for the police. The poets were outnumbered, and both of them ended up with their arms pinned behind them and drinks poured over them.

They were brought before Trungpa who argued that they had asked to come to his seminary and therefore should abide by his rules. Merwin replied that an interest in Buddhist teaching should not entail enslavement to it. Tom Clark's "The Great Naropa Poetry Wars" and Ed Sanders's "The Party" both give fuller accounts of the dispute, but what is for certain is that Trungpa ordered that the poets be stripped. As Merwin recalled, "He ordered his guards to do the job. They dragged us apart, and it was then that Dana started screaming. Several of them on each of us, holding us down . . . ` Naome was also assaulted: "Guards dragged me off and pinned me to the floor . . . I fought and called to friends, men and women whose faces I saw in the crowd, to call the police. No one did . . . The rest of my clothes were torn off."

The two poets stood before Trungpa, humiliated, beaten and naked.

The incident tarnished the whole community, inciting rumors about megalomania and brainwashing, and a climate of suspicion and hostility descended upon Naropa, only made worse by Trungpa's refusal to apologize. Ginsberg's loyalties were inevitably divided, as he was asked to pledge his allegiance to either poetry or his guru. As one journal entry put it: "trapped 'like smoke going down bamboo tube' between Poesy and Dharma, Merwin and Trungpa, in their ghost war. Hypocrite, I take rides with each. I haven't pursued my prostrations. I push and preach Dharma and poetry in public. I can't face Merwin, I get angry at my boyfriends and students, I am a hairy loss."

The affair dragged on. The National Endowment for the Arts had caught wind of the incident and rejected two applications to fund the Kerouac Poetics School. By 1977 most of the poetry faculty were being paid directly from Ginsberg's own pocket. The poet Robert Bly coined the term "Buddhist fascism" and greater pressure was placed upon Ginsberg to disown his teacher and support his fellow poets.

To make matters worse, Ed Sanders's course on "Investigative Poetics" decided to make the incident the subject of its study, and twenty-four students turned detective, interviewing everybody who had been connected with the evening. Trungpa did not help his cause by refusing to be interviewed. Furthermore, he had taken to being chauffeured around in a Mercedes-Benz and insisted on being addressed as "Sir" by students who he was beginning to treat like servants. He surrounded himself with bodyguards and was behaving erratically, convinced of his own grandeur.

Ginsberg continued to play go-between, although the findings of Sanders's students were highly critical of Trungpa. The poet Ed Dorn got hold of a copy of their report and began distributing it amongst the artistic community. Ferlinghetti approached Ginsberg for a copy but was refused.

The press began their own investigations, suspecting that Trungpa was a self-appointed leader of a sinister cult. *Harper's* magazine ran a feature, while the local paper, the *Daily Camera,* ran an editorial which urged, "To Avoid the Name, Shed the Disguise." Tom Clark interviewed Ginsberg for the *Boulder Monthly*. He defended Trungpa's motives, accusing the poetic community of hypocrisy: "Burroughs commits murder, Gregory Corso borrows money from everybody and shoots up drugs for twenty years but he's 'divine Gregory,' but poor old Trungpa, who's been suffering since he was two years old to teach the Dharma, isn't allowed to wave *his* frankfurter. And if he does, the poets get real mad that their territory is being invaded."

Ginsberg's comments incensed other writers. The publisher Bob Callahan called for a

According to Mel Howard, "Allen saw Dylan rightly connected to the whole tradition of the Beat generation and through that to the earlier poets." (© Elsa Dorfman.)

boycott of the School of Disembodied Poetics until Trungpa's empire had been disbanded. A petition in support of Callahan received the signatures of many writers, including Ishmael Reed, David Henderson and Jim Pepper. Rexroth angrily announced that "Trungpa has unquestionably done more harm to Buddhism in the United States than any man living."

Only Snyder and Michael McClure defended Trungpa, although their stance seems more designed to protect Ginsberg.

By the end of the seventies, both Clark and Sanders had published their accounts of the Naropa war. The clash

On July 8, 1976 Louis Ginsberg died peacefully in his sleep. On his way to bury his father, Ginsberg composed the poem "Father Death Blues." (© Joe Zimel.)

had taken on national proportions, with reports of sexual scandal, financial corruption and dictatorial teaching stretching from the West Coast's *Berkeley Barb* to New York's *Soho Weekly News*. Accusations of improper funding from the National Endowment for the Arts (N.E.A.) jeopardized literature subsidies in general. Grants for the St. Mark's Poetry Project and L.A.'s Beyond Baroque were seriously diminished. As late as 1985, a group of Republicans attempted to force Congress to withdraw funding from Peter Orlovsky's book *Clean Asshole Poems and Smiling Vegetable Songs*.

The damage that the Merwin–Trungpa affair inflicted upon Ginsberg cannot be underestimated. For a man who had prided himself on the introduction of like-minded thinkers, he had finally become a victim of cross-fire. It caused him to doubt his allegiance to friends, poetry and religion alike. "I've difficulty knowing whether I'm lying to myself to cover Trungpa's hierarchical secrecy," he confided to his journal, "or lying to [Tom] Clark in not openly and continuously confronting him in his journalistic spitefulness and intrigue. This inhibits my writing altogether since I don't want to waste my poesy and readers' time on gossip and spite, or exhibit my own confusion."

Chapter

10

Previous page: Ginsberg and
Lawrence Ferlinghetti.
(© Gene Anthony.)
This page: Ginsberg and Robert
Lowell.
(© Martin Rechellblatt.)

Despite the scandal at Naropa, Ginsberg continued to move towards the center of the literary establishment. In 1974 his *The Fall of America* won the National Book Award in Poetry. By 1979 he had become a member of the National Arts Club whom he thanked for giving him "approval on cocksucking by the commissioner of cultural affairs." Most prestigious of all, in 1974 he had been made a member of the American Academy and Institute of Arts and Letters – an honor that Burroughs would receive nearly a decade later.

Yet for all the recognition, the creative momentum of Ginsberg's work was increasingly questioned. He continued to tour, but his performances were inclined to be as formulaic as they had once been electric. The critic Charles Molesworth may have praised "Ginsberg's reading voice [as] an extremely pleasurable instrument that at its best seems to partake of the structural complexity of an Eastern raga and the improvizational push of jazz," but at the same time, this focus on his voice begs the question of the quality of the work that it was reciting.

The journalist Mark Shechner similarly remarked: "At this stage of the game, rather than try to push ahead poetically, Ginsberg has taken to doubling back upon himself, and the journals, correspondence, memoirs and *obiter dicta* . . . that now tumble onto the market suggest that what we can henceforth look forward to are neither breakthroughs nor refinements in poetry, but Ginsberg's efforts to clarify his image and carve out a place in American cultural history. One suspects that Ginsberg understands these days that he matters less as a poet than as a figure . . . Certainly he has grown influential without being consistently great, or even consistently engaging as a writer, and most of us can count on one hand the poems that survive rereading, let alone study."

At yet another reading at Columbia University, *Time* magazine reported that "he talks with the measured deliberation of a statesman-celebrity . . .

"Something has changed. This puckish little figure, this professorial imp with the loony grin, does not sound angry. He is not wailing about the wickedness of his time. He is mocking the past – mocking the angry radicals, mocking the dreamers, mocking the quest for visions. The audience is laughing with him. They are howling, but in pleasure rather than anger, as he thrusts an arm up for each of the jokes."

The Kerouac conference's list of speakers read like a bohemian Who's Who, and included Merry Prankster Ken Kesey and Ginsberg, among others. (© John Teton.)

With a sense of resigned ennui, the review concluded: "In Europe, where 100,000 Prague students once elected Ginsberg King of the May, the young are once again marching against war. On campuses there are teach-ins about the threat of nuclear holocaust. But this night, at this Columbia campus, sartorially and spiritually the most volatile and un-Ivy of the Ivy League, Allen Ginsberg is chatting, singing, wearing a necktie and making his howl a thigh-slapping hoot. His last words are prophetic, but not in the stirring way of the years gone by. He plays a worn squeeze-box and sings: 'Meditate on emptiness, 'cause that's where you're going, and how.'"

Certainly Ginsberg felt himself to be blocked – the Reagan era ushered in a climate that saw no place for the poet's mystic politics.

His personal life had not been made any easier by his decision to look after Burroughs's son. "Your cursed from birth offspring" was how Billy Jr. once signed off a letter to his father, and with good reason. Owing to his mother's drug consumption when pregnant, he had been born addicted to speed and alcohol, and the first week of his life was spent undergoing withdrawal. As his friend John Steinbeck Jr. later wrote, "The first liver cell he ever owned was hard put

Ginsberg, Stewart Brand, and Peter Orlovsky at Whole Earth Day, 1978. Ginsberg continued to appear at public events and performances, though it was questioned whether he was important as a poet or simply as a figure. (© Larry Keenan, Jr.)

Ginsberg's performances were increasingly considered to be formulaic where they had once been eclectic, and the creative momentum of his output was under constant scrutiny.
(© Lisa Law.)

to mesoderm its way into helpfulness. Speed and booze were a constant birthday present when you look at it that way." In adulthood Billy drank with a painful abandon, virtually living the life of a derelict. Ginsberg pulled some strings and, after a detox in Santa Cruz, Billy became a teaching assistant at Naropa. His sobriety was short-lived. By August 1976 he had to be admitted to Denver General where he lapsed into a six-day coma. Being the only hospital in the country to perform liver transplants, he was lucky enough to be provided with a donor.

In January 1977 Billy was discharged from the hospital, armed with prescriptions for steroids and tranquillizers. He punished his new liver with the same ferocity that had destroyed his old one. Anne Waldman recalled his "haunting and harried presence as his condition worsened . . . Giving away money [his father had given him], befriending stray people, cats and dogs, collecting garbage (anything was salvageable) . . . wearing his heart and his wounds on his sleeve."

January 10, 1973

Dear Mr. Ginsberg:

I have the honor and pleasure to inform you that announcement will shortly be made of your election to the National Institute of Arts and Letters as a member of the Department of Literature. New members will be invited to attend an informal dinner on Wednesday, April 4th, but formal induction will take place at our public ceremonial, to be held on May 16, 1973 at three o'clock, at which time you will receive the insignia of the Institute.

Will you be kind enough to let us know at your earliest convenience that you accept this election? We will release the story of the 1973 elections to the press upon receipt of the acceptances, so I would ask you to keep the news of your election confidential at the present time.

Sincerely yours,

Joseph Mitchell
Secretary

P.S.    Enclosed is a list of members and a brochure describing the Institute.

Please verify your address for inclusion in the forthcoming Yearbook for 1973, and send us four glossy photographs.

Mr. Allen Ginsberg
170 East 2 Street, Apt. 16
New York, N.Y.  10009

In 1974 Ginsberg was made a member of the American Academy and Institute of Arts and Letters. (Courtesy of the American Academy and Institute of Arts and Letters.)

The next four years would be a depressing litany of hospitalizations, psychiatric treatment and failed abstentionism. On March 2, 1981 he was found collapsed in a ditch by the side of a road in DeLand, Florida, and died in hospital early the next day. He was thirty-three years old.

Throughout this time Ginsberg had played nurse, counselor and surrogate mother. He took the funeral arrangements upon himself, opting for a Buddhist ceremony at the Rocky Mountain Dharma Center. Burroughs stayed in New York while Ginsberg chanted, "Form is emptiness, emptiness is form" over the young man's urn.

If his poetic muse was less accessible than it had been, Ginsberg found outlets elsewhere. He continued to teach at Naropa. giving lectures on the Beats, seminars on Blake, and introducing his students to the work of William Carlos Williams. Unfortunately, this was not all he was introducing them to. As he told the *Washington Post* in February 1981: "I believe the best teaching is done in bed, and I am informed that's the classical tradition. That the present prohibitive and unnatural separation between student and teacher may be some twentieth-century Wowser, Moral Majority, un-American obsession. The great example of teaching was Socrates . . . It's healthy and appropriate for the student and the teacher to have a love relationship whenever possible . . . I think it should be institutionally encouraged . . . My own experience is that a certain kind of genius among students is best brought out in bed."

Ginsberg's sexual politics are a sticking point for even his most devoted of fans. At one point he became a member of N.A.M.B.L.A. (National Association for Man-Boy Love – the American equivalent of England's Pedophile Information Exchange), arguing that those with an interest in "inter-generational love" were victims of ignorant persecution. There is certainly no evidence that Ginsberg abused or bribed any of his boy-students, although a writer like Andrew Vachss would be quick to point out that the intrinsic power relationship between adolescent and adult is axiomatically abusive once it becomes sexual. Alternatively, Miles has suggested that, "Allen was indulging in hyperbole in citing Socrates and his active recommendation of teacher-student love, just to shock."

"It was always a free-speech issue," explains Rosenthal, his secretary, "Allen was never a pedophile."

Whatever the reading, Ginsberg's brazen acknowledgement of his fondness for pubescent boys still casts a shadow over his image as

Ernesto Cardenal at the poetry festival in support of national liberation in Nicaragua.
(© Allen Ginsberg Trust.)

"free love" advocate.

During his vacation from Boulder, Ginsberg continued to travel. His first stop was Mexico City and a writers' conference that also boasted Gunter Grass and Jorge Louis Borges. The eighty-two-year-old Borges mistook Ginsberg for his father, although they did manage a cordial exchange of views on the merits of Pound.

After a brief return to America (where he provided guest vocals for The Clash's album *Combat Rock*), Ginsberg moved on to Nicaragua. A poetry festival had been organized in support of national liberation. The Sandinista government felt that an American invasion was not unlikely, and Ginsberg consulted with Commandante Ortega to ensure he did not feed into any imperialist propaganda. His reading was simultaneously translated into Spanish, and included poems such as "America," "Elegy Che Guevara," and the defiantly political "Birdbrain!": "Birdbrain supplied helicopters to Central American generals, kill a lot of/restless Indians, encourage a favorable business climate." He was received with some caution and much delight.

Ginsberg was inspired by the progress that had been made by the Sandinistas. He denounced the anti-government newspaper *La Prensa* as a C.I.A. front, and gave press conferences arguing that it was American intervention, and not the revolution, that was jeopardizing personal freedom. Along with the Russian poet Yevgeny Yevtushenko, he prepared a statement calling upon "the world's writers to come to Nicaragua to see with their own eyes the reality of Nicaragua, and lift their voices in defense of this country, small but inspired. They'll be welcome and can acquaint themselves directly with the true character of this revolution, of the efforts of the people to create a just society exempt from violence, a revolution whose image is being consciously distorted by those who have an interest in destroying the alternative which it proposes."

Compared to his visit to Cuba, his time in Central America displayed a greater political maturity. He did not foreground his own platform – pot and homosexuality – but seemed more willing to accept and defend the one that the Sandinistas were trying to erect. On his return to the States he would continue to speak out in support of Nicaragua, giving a stream of interviews supporting the rebels and denouncing C.I.A.-backed involvement.

Back in Boulder, Naropa's poetry department was planning a Kerouac conference – a media event that would coincide with the twenty-fifth anniversary of *On the Road's* publication. The list of conferees read like a bohemian Who's Who, ranging from Corso, Creeley, McClure and Bremser through Carl Solomon, Huncke, Clellon Holmes, and

**Overleaf: Ginsberg and Russian poet Yevgeny Yevtushenko, who together had prepared a statement calling for "the world's writers to come to Nicaragua to see with their own eyes the reality."**
(© **Gene Anthony.**)

Burroughs to Kesey, Abbie Hoffman, and Timothy Leary. The event received national attention: T.V., radio, the press and even a documentary film-maker turned up to witness the canonization of St. Jack.

As with Ginsberg's own performances, the event was more an act of wistful nostalgia than it was a battle-plan for the future. There is an antiquated flavor in all of the accounts, a sense that the writers present belonged to a residual rather than an emergent culture.

Celebrity and reputation were fast becoming Ginsberg's currency, and touring was the best way to capitalize upon it.

No sooner had he wrapped up the Kerouac tribute than he began preparing for a three-month tour of Europe. In December he played "War on War" at Paris, followed quickly by the One World Poetry tour of Holland. Copenhagen was followed by Stockholm, then on to Helsinki and back to Norway. The final gig of the tour took place in Wuppertal, Germany, and was filmed, later to be released as the video *Allen Ginsberg on Tour.*

As if the road was not taxing enough, matters were made worse by Orlovsky's

Jean Michel Basquait, Burroughs, and Ginsberg at Burroughs's New York studio "The Bunker." Ginsberg's personal life had not been made easier by his decision to look after Burroughs's son. (© Victor Bockris.)

Celebrity and reputation were fast becoming Ginsberg's currency, and touring was the best way to capitalize on it. (© Lisa Law.)

deteriorating mental state. His father had died the previous November, leaving him with the pressure of looking after his family. His behavior veered between the obsessive and the manic – wailing, compulsive cleaning and excessive drinking. He spurned Ginsberg's concern and grew more isolated by the day. At a reading in Amsterdam he punctuated each of his lines of verse by hitting himself on the head. He was convinced, perhaps not unrealistically, that Reagan was out to get him, and would spend days mumbling barely audible conspiracy theories. (When Ginsberg's name appeared on a 1984 United States Information "blacklist," Orlovsky proved that his fears were well grounded.) Orlovsky's paranoia may have had substance, but his drinking was an ongoing problem, and it was to Ginsberg's enormous relief that they completed the tour.

In an attempt to settle himself, Ginsberg returned to teaching and found himself an agent, Andrew Wylie. Between the financial security that Wylie established for him and with the future of Naropa ensured, Ginsberg was able to return to New York. It was here that he assembled the final draft of his *Collected Poems 1947–80.*

While waiting for it to be published, he and Snyder were invited to China as part of a poetry-exchange programme. They arrived in Beijing late in 1984 to attend a conference entitled "The Source of Inspiration." Ginsberg expressed surprise at the fluency the Chinese writers displayed in American letters. He found himself cited alongside Whitman and Eliot as an inspiration for the poetry of Yuan Kejia; clearly his work had struck a chord with the hosts who had witnessed the cultural revolution. As he later observed in "Reading Bai Juyi":

I learned that the Great Leap Forward caused millions of families to starve, that the anti-Rightist Campaign against bourgeois "Stinkers" sent revolutionary poets to shovel shit in Xinjiang Province a decade before the Cultural Revolution drove countless millions of readers to cold huts and starvation in the countryside Northwest.

The conference lasted four days and was followed by a sight-seeing tour through Xi'an, Shangai and Canton. Instead of returning after it had finished, Ginsberg stole some time to give lectures on the Beats in Beijing and on Whitman at Hebei University in Boading. His lecture stint was over by December and he noted a "farewell that was warm with typsy embraces."

Chapter

11

Previous page: Ginsberg reading in
Washington Square Park, N.Y.C.
(© Kaoru Sekine.)
This page: In 1986 Brooklyn College
made Ginsberg a professor.
(© Lisa Law.)

Ginsberg's return to the States coincided with the appearance of reviews for his collection of poems. Notices for the book were mixed, although the sheer number of them testify to its significance. *Time* magazine somewhat superciliously heralded "The Mainstreaming of Allen Ginsberg," although the *Inquirer* warmed to his "record of life in postwar America, a map of his slowly evolving spiritual awareness and a frame-by-frame picaresque documentary starring the gamboling self in modern society." *New Republic* argued that "these 800 pages prove . . . that Ginsberg has always been a minor poet." (The fact that the journal dedicated three pages to its argument could be said to contradict its thesis.)

Brooklyn College certainly did not share this opinion and, in 1986, made him a distinguished professor. His duties amounted to a seminar, a literature class and tutorials each semester and provided him with enough money for him to be more selective about his performances. It was a post that Ginsberg relished, maintaining it until the year of his death and playfully parodying it in poems such as "Personal Ad" and "Return of Kral Majales."

Greater stability allowed him to pursue his interest in photography. He had always been a keen amateur, and indeed one of his collections was deposited at Columbia and famously re-surfaced in Ann Charter's "Scenes Along the Road." By the late eighties he was taking it more seriously, allowing himself to be guided by professionals such as Berenice Abbott and Robert Frank. He also collaborated with John Cage, and his work graced the pages of magazines such as *Vanity Fair* and *Aperture*. Photography was in many ways an extension of his poetry – both art forms welded together by an aesthetic of the moment. At once personal and public, leisurely and frozen, his photography shares with his poetry an ability to make the familiar mythic. In *On Photography*, Susan Sontag remarked: "To photograph is to confer importance. There is probably no object that cannot be beautified; moreover, there is no way to suppress the

**Ginsberg and Burroughs at Burroughs's eightieth birthday party. (© Victor Bockris.)**

tendency inherent in all photographs to accord value to their subjects . . . In the open fields of American experience, as cataloged with passion by Whitman and as sized up with a shrug by Warhol, everybody is a celebrity  No moment is more important than any other moment; no person is more interesting than any other person."

If Ginsberg's poetry echoes Whitman's "Song of Myself," his photography could be said to resonate with his "Democratic Vistas." When asked by the poet Jim Moore if "the impulse to take photographs come(s) from the same place as to write," Ginsberg replied, "More or less, noticing the moment and space, the visual moment. Yes, it is very similar. I

notice carrying a camera around habitually now, which I've done since 1984, I tend to write less in my pocket notebook. I take photographs of things that otherwise I would make verbal descriptions of . . . I come back to the photographs and then I write captions, extensive captions on them; they're like haikus . . . It's like family photos: they're really there . . . There's always something. If you gave it to a really good printmaker it could be something

In February 1988, Ginsberg collaborated with Philip Glass on a musical version of "Wichita Vortex." (© Fred W. McDarrah.)

This page and overleaf: Early in 1988 Ginsberg attended a demonstration in Tel Aviv to protest against the treatment of Palestinians in the occupied territories, and in front of a crowd of 60,000 people he read "Jaweh and Allah Battle." (© Allen Ginsberg Trust.)

they could put in the Museum of Modern Art."

They did. His first show, "Hideous Human Angels," opened at the Holly Solomon Gallery in New York in 1985, and was followed by exhibitions in Washington, Dallas and Boston.

As well as photography, Ginsberg continued to explore his musical outlets. In February of 1988, he collaborated with the composer Philip Glass on a musical version of "Wichita Vortex." It was performed at the Shubert Theatre in New York, and in many ways was an ideal coupling: Glass's minimalism foregrounded the hypnotic variations to be

רוצים שלום -
עכשיו
טוב שלום
מארץ ישראל
שלמה
2 מדינות
2 מדינות
שלום
ישראל
שלמה

Ginsberg, Vaclav Havel and Nanao Sakaki at the Majales celebration in Prague, 1990.
(© Jaroslav Kratochvil.)

found in monotone – an aesthetic that can be traced back to the repetitive incantations of Ginsberg's lists and litanies.

In general, the poet's performances may have become less frequent, but they regained their intensity. Perhaps the apotheosis of Ginsberg's spoken word career came six months before his death, at New York's St. Mark's Poetry Project. To celebrate his *Selected Poems: 1947–1995*, the project brought together an impressively disparate array of musicians. Sonic Youth's Lee Ranaldo, the Pixies' Kim Deal, and the guitarist Lenny Kaye were among the rock stars who accompanied his reading. That the seventy-year-old poet could still hold such appeal for a generation twice removed speaks volumes about Ginsberg's iconic resilience, his feel for the contemporary even as he acknowledges his distance from it. The self-styled Rimbaud of rock, Patti Smith, has long acknowledged her debt to both Ginsberg and Burroughs – her mesmeric "babelogues" paying homage to a tradition of the "American artist [who has] no guilt" and whose intention is to reawaken "the nerves under your skin." Beck, the self-proclaimed "Loser" and Dylan of the M.T.V. generation, also became a friend and was cited regularly by Ginsberg as one of the keepers of his flame. His last C.D. boasted the music of Paul McCartney, as well as Glass and Marc Ribot. "The Ballad of the Skeletons" would be his last recording – a diatribe against corporate America because, as he told *The New York Times*, "Somebody's got to stand up to those idiots!"

Stances were indeed something he had continued to take. Early in 1988 he attended a demonstration in Tel Aviv to protest against the treatment of Palestinians in the occupied territories. In front of a crowd of some 60,000 people he read "Jaweh and Allah Battle" – a poem that uncovered the plague that lay in both houses of the conflict:

Both Gods Terrible! Awful Jaweh Allah!
Both hook-nosed gods, circumcised.
Jaweh Allah which unreal?

Which stronger Illusion?

Which stronger Army?

Which gives most frightening command?

Along with Sontag, Mailer, Erica Jong and Arthur Miller, Ginsberg became involved with the plight of writers who were opposed to the Israeli government's behavior on the West Bank. A letter drafted by the P.E.N. Freedom-To-Write Committee urged the Israeli government "to end its policy of arrests of Palestinian and Israeli journalists, to reopen censored Palestinian newspapers, to reopen the Palestinian Press Service, and to cease its practice of censorship of books, school reading materials, newspapers and literary texts circulated in the West Bank and the Gaza Territories."

Despite opposition from the pro-Israeli lobby, and disapproval from some of his friends, Ginsberg was one of the letter's signatories. For all his apparent contradictions, one of Ginsberg's constants was his commitment to freedom of expression.

Censorship was an issue that had once more returned to haunt Ginsberg's own work. In 1987, the Federal Communications Commission restricted the broadcast of "indecent" material to a so-called "safe harbor" period between 10 p.m. and 6 a.m. Their thinking was that such a watershed would minimize the risk of minors being exposed to "obscenities" such as "Howl." That bastion of Republicanism, Jesse Helms (a "rightwing-fear-mongering-tobacco-pushing-chicken-necked cracker", according to the ever-astute Bill Hicks) pushed through legislation that extended the ban around the clock. The issue was bounced back and forth between the Supreme Court, the F.C.C. and the Court of Appeals until the safe harbor period was once more established: "And tho I am King of May my howls & proclamations present are banned/by F.C.C. on America's electric airwaves 6 AM to midnight," he wrote in "Return of Kral Majales".

What made the F.C.C.'s decision all the more insidious was that it refused to judge in advance what it considered obscene, passing judgement only after the material has been broadcast. In other words, broadcasters could not risk breaking the law, because they did not know if they were doing so. As Eric Lieberman,

**Vaclav Havel reading Ginsberg's "Kral Majales" for the first time. (© Jaroslav Kratochvil.)**

Ginsberg at the F.F.C.'s Bar Association
forum, where he read a list of works
that had been affected by the F.F.C.'s
censorship legislation.
(© Ursula B. Day.)

Ginsberg's New York attorney said, "[Indecency] means what a majority of F.C.C. commissioners come to determine it means after the fact." At a 1990 forum of the F.C.C.'s Bar Association, Ginsberg read a list of works that had also been affected, including Albee's *Who's Afraid of Virginia Woolf?*, Baldwin's *Another Country*, Kundera's *The Unbearable Lightness of Being*, and Mailer's *The Naked and the Dead.* "While we have glasnost slowly approaching in Eastern Europe," Ginsberg told the commission, "We seem to have a crackdown on a very large scale on communication of a spiritual, personal, and straightforward candid nature within the United States."

Forty years after Judge Horn declared that "Howl" was not obscene, but in fact "a plea for holy living," the battle still rages on via America's airwaves. "I'm simply trying to write according to the directions of Walt Whitman, who said he hoped the poets of the future would specialize in candor. I'm trying to record my experiences candidly, and that right must be protected because my experiences are more or less parallel with other people's," Ginsberg had said, stating emphatically, "It really is book burning. Censorship [is] thought control."

At the time of writing, any daytime broadcast of "Howl" – a poem that is one of the most widely anthologized works in American letters – is forbidden by law. Ginsberg's verse still belongs to the midnight hours.

Chapter

12

Orlovsky's story, meanwhile, was one of dramatic decline. By the mid-eighties, his drinking had reached the point where it was self-medication and poison both. Eventually he was hospitalized after a particularly erratic incident in which he threatened Ginsberg's secretary, Bob Rosenthal, and then mutilated himself. Still he continued to drink and, for the safety of both Ginsberg and himself, they separated – Ginsberg attending an Al-Anon programme in Minneapolis, Orlovsky moving to one of Trungpa's retreats in Vermont. Friends found Orlovsky difficult to be around, referring to him with both immense affection and deep despair.

"Peter suffered from mental illness

Previous page: Ginsberg playing the harmonium.
(© Allen Ginsberg Trust.)
This page: Ginsberg and his assistant, Bob Rosenthal, in their New York office.
(© Lisa Law.)

caused by decades of substance abuse," says Rosenthal. "He has a bi-polar personality and was in and out of hospital all through the late eighties and early nineties . . . It put an incredible strain on Allen, he spent a lot of time and energy in dealing with doctors and social workers." That said, their bond remained solid and Orlovsky has managed to remain out of hospital for the last three years, and was sober for the year before Ginsberg died.

Ginsberg continued to tour and travel throughout the nineties. Indeed, the media-interest in him increased from around 1992 onwards, with more and more requests for interviews, film appearances, book offers and reading gigs. "It was something that he loved to do," recalls Rosenthal, "It was a great joy for him and probably one of the last things that he wanted to cut out." It was also his main source of income, for it was not until 1994 that Ginsberg truly became financially settled by selling off his letters, journals, photographs and memorabilia to Stanford University for $1 million.

Ginsberg has been much criticized for the Stanford sale, receiving snide critiques about how the icon of the counter-culture turned himself into an over-the-counter-

The sale of his material allowed Ginsberg to move to a palatial apartment on East 13th Street.
(© Sid Kaplan.)

Ginsberg fell into a coma just one week after he received diagnosis of his illness. He died in a hospital bed positioned where this photograph of his own bed was taken from. (© Sid Kaplan.)

product. Yet for forty years Ginsberg had subsidized writers, friends and campaigns. He gave as many benefit readings as he did those for his own gain, and certainly Naropa could not have continued without his generous help. For a lifetime's dedication to poetry, politics and publishing, the $1 million seems an almost modest award – especially when one considers that 50 per cent went straight to the I.R.S., and that a sizeable portion of that was taken up with various causes and outlays.

What the sale did allow him to do was move from 437 East 12th St. (an apartment he had kept on throughout his peripatetic lifestyle) to a more palatial loft on East 13th St.

Naropa remained another constant in Ginsberg's life, with him paying regular visits there at least twice a year. On his way back to New York he would usually stop off in Lawrence, Kansas where Burroughs was living a semi-retired life, focusing more on painting than writing. "Allen was such a workaholic," recalls James Grauerholz, Burroughs's secretary, "that he found Lawrence very restful. He would usually spend a week or two here, living with Bill and being taken care of by our Lawrence family." In November 1996, there was a symposium on Burroughs's "Ports of Entry" exhibition that was due to open at the University of Kansas. Ginsberg attended and stayed on for a little while longer. It would be the last time the two men met each other face to face, their subsequent conversations being confined to regular telephone calls.

On April 3, 1997, "Wired News" reported that, "Allen Ginsberg . . . has been diagnosed with hepatocellular carcinoma, cancer of the liver. The cancer is untreatable, and the poet has 'four to twelve' months to live, says his doctor, David Clain, of Beth Israel Medical Center." The diagnosis was the culmination of a long series of ailments. On his trip to South America, when he was just twenty-five, he had contracted hepatitis and so had

lived the majority of his adult life with a liver impairment. By 1988 the hepatitis (A, B and C) had developed into cirrhosis, and by the nineties he was also known to be suffering from diabetes and congestive heart failure. According to Rosenthal, "These were the symptoms that were most bothering him on a daily basis. He went on a macro-biotic diet and saw a heart doctor in Boston. Then from February of 1997 onwards, he just went

Among those present at Ginsberg's bedside were Gregory Corso and Patti Smith. (© Greg Masters.)

down-hill health-wise, and got weaker and weaker. The cardiologist finally couldn't help. I had him taken into Beth Israel Hospital on the emergency ward. I arranged that he could be taken right in, and it was here that he got the final diagnosis . . . I don't think it was a bad thing. There was nothing that would have saved him, no life-saving procedures like a liver transplant . . . Liver cancer has no pain associated with it, so we knew he would just go into a coma and that would be it. There would be no suffering."

On his release from hospital he rang as many of his friends as he could. Being Ginsberg, it was a massive list, and he made literally hundreds of calls, weeping with some people, confiding to Burroughs that, "I thought I would be terrified, in fact I am exhilarated." He wrote furiously, his last work being a poem entitled "Things I'll Not Do."

On Thursday, April 3 Rosenthal had to slip out of the apartment. He asked Ginsberg if

Twenty-four hours after his death, Ginsberg's body was moved to the Shambhala Center, and was cremated the following Tuesday in New Jersey. Gelek Rinpoche was among the speakers at the Shambhala Center funeral.
(© Paula Litzky.)

he wanted to go back to sleep. "Oh, yes," was the reply. They were the last words his assistant heard him speak. When he returned, Ginsberg was in a sleep that led to a coma – it had been a week since he received the diagnosis.

Like his life, Ginsberg's death was an eminently public affair, with friends and spiritual gurus holding a vigil by his bedside. Patti Smith, Bill Morgan, Peter Hale, Andrew Wylie and Roy Lichtenstein were just some of those present. Rose "Rosebud" Pettet, a friend for more than thirty years, was also there and wrote a moving account of his final hours: "Allen lay in a narrow hospital bed beside the windows overlooking 14th Street. There were two almost invisible tubes coming out of his nose, attached to a portable small oxygen tank on the floor. His head was raised up on a couple of big striped pillows and he looked tiny and frail, thin arms with bruised veins from hospital tests sticking out from his Jewell Heart T-shirt. Head to the side, slight shadows under the eyes. I had walked through the loft, people whispering greetings, hugging, telling me all that had happened. But still not really prepared for the sight of him . . . An altar had been set up along one side of the loft and Gelek Rinpoche [Ginsberg's Buddhist teacher] and the other monks sat chanting and praying, the sound so soothing constantly in the background, bells tinkling."

It was around 11 p.m. on the Friday night, and no one knew how long he would last. Corso had his picture taken with him, Orlovsky was taking others. They tried to joke that this is exactly what their dying friend would have done.

Pettet continues: "The loft was very quiet. Most were resting, half-asleep. Suddenly Allen began to shake, a small convulsion wracked his body . . . It was about 2.15. Joel [Ginsberg's cousin and doctor] examined him, pulse, etc., and said that his vital signs were considerably slower, he had had another seizure. The breathing went on, weaker. His feet were cooler. Everyone sat or stood close to the little bed, stroking and kissing him softly.

The ceremony was as much a celebration of Ginsberg's life as a mourning for his death. (© Paula Litzky.)

This page and opposite: Ginsberg's death was reported on virtually every television and radio station in America and Europe. A year later, a public tribute was held at St. John the Divine, N.Y.C.
(© Lisa Law.)

Peter Orlovsky bent over and kissed his head saying, "Good-bye, Darling."

"Suddenly then a remarkable thing happened. A tremor went through him, and slowly, impossibly, be began to raise his head. He weakly tried to sit up, and his left arm lifted and extended. Then his eyes opened very slowly and very wide. The pupils were wildly dilated . . . His head began to turn very slowly and his eyes seemed to glance around him, gazing on each of us in turn . . . His mouth opened, and we all heard as he seemed to struggle to say something, but only a soft low sound, a weak 'Aaah' came from him. Then his eyes began to close and he sank back weakly onto the pillow. The eyes shut fully . . .

"At 2.39, Joel checked for vital signs and announced that the heart, so much stronger than anyone knew, had stopped beating. A painless and gentle death. The thin blue sheet was pulled up to his chin, and Peter Hale brought over a tiny cup and spoon, and placed a few drops of a dark liquid between Allen's lips. It was part of the Buddhist ritual – the "last food." Bob put his hand over Allen's eyes and said the Sh'ma. We all sat quietly in the dim light, each with our own thoughts, saying good-bye."

As Ginsberg's corpse lay in repose, his friend the poet Ann Waldman composed some "Notes on Sitting Beside A Nobel Corpse":

Light
Breeze
Stirring the Curtains, Blue – Faint Tremor of
His Blue Shroud

which ended with the lament:

Full Century's brilliant Allen's gone, in other myraid forms live on
See through this palpable skull's tender eye, kind mind kind mind
don't die!

Buddhist practice prohibited the
moving of the body until the

consciousness had meditated itself out. It would be twenty hours before Ginsberg's corpse was moved to the Shambhala Center, and it was cremated the following Tuesday in New Jersey. Although no one was present at the actual cremation, a ceremony was held beforehand at which people could pay their respects. Waldman, Amiri Baraka (LeRoi Jones) and Orlovsky all spoke, and the event was as much a celebration of his life as a mourning for his death.

"The ashes were divided," says Rosenthal. "One portion went to be poured into the foundation of a rest area at the Rocky Mountain Shambhala Center in Colorado. An equal portion was given to Galek Rinpoche. The rest of the ashes we buried in the family plot in Elizabeth New Jersey right next to his father."

He has a Jewish stone, and a Jewish unveiling took place in the spring of 1998.

His death made the front page of *The New York Times*. He was "a great loss to me and to everybody," Burroughs told them: "We were friends for more than fifty years. Allen was a great person with a worldwide influence. He was a pioneer of openness and a lifelong model of candor."

*The New York Times* was not alone. Ginsberg's death was reported on virtually every television and radio station in America and Europe. Newspapers afforded it the kind of coverage usually reserved for senior statesmen – an appropriate response as, in many ways, that is exactly what he was. Poems were written, songs performed, vigils held.

Tributes to him were held in places as far apart as Chicago and London, Stockholm and Berlin. St. Mark's Church, Ginsberg's poetic home, held a service which included Corso, Orlovsky, Joyce Johnson, Hal Wilner, Ron

This page and opposite: Among the performers at the tribute were Johnny Depp, Gregory Corso and Robert Hasse (© Lisa Law.)

Padgett and Lou Reed. Patti Smith sang Hank Williams's "I'm So Lonesome I Could Cry." At the Temple Emanu-El in San Francisco, more than 2,000 people poured in to say their goodbyes. Michael McClure rubbed shoulders with Dennis Hopper, former Mayor Joe Alioto shared his grief with the U.S. poet Laureate Robert Hass. Ferlinghetti read "Allen Ginsberg Dying," a work which finishes:

Here by the sea
in San Francisco
where the waves weep
They make a sibilant sound
a sibylline sound
*Allen* they whisper
*Allen.*

Joanne Kyger, Diane Di Prima, and Gary Snyder, all joined in with retired professors, ageing hippies and students for whom "Howl" was now a set-text.

There were dozens of laments and thousands of words of remembrance. Yet perhaps

Hass captured the mood most acutely when he chose not to read from his own work, but returned instead to a letter that William Carlos Williams had sent to Ezra Pound: "Whatever you want to call him, hidden under as fine a heap of crap as you'll find blossoming on our city dump-heaps, is a sensitive mind. I like him in spite of myself."

Patti Smith, Oliver Ray, and J.D. Daugherty performing at Ginsberg's tribute in 1998. (© Allen Ginsberg Trust.)

# Afterword

A new play about "The Kerouac Connection" premièred at the 1997 Edinburgh Festival. Later the same year, a film entitled *House of America* explored how a group of dispossessed Welsh adolescents live vicariously though Beat mythology. The 1998 movie *The Last Time I Committed Suicide* is a dramatized version of one of Neal Cassady's self-revelatory letters. *Naked Lunch* has been filmed by no less a figure than David Cronenberg. Beat fanzines and websites boast tens of thousands of subscribers. A film of *On The Road* is rumored to be in production. Beat anthologies and critical commentaries are an industry unto themselves. Courses on "The Beats" are now a standard option for most universities who teach American Literature.

The current upsurge of interest in all things Beat may say more about our own times than it does about the writers themselves. They certainly grabbed the gray-flannel suits of the fifties and stripped them of their self-satisfied comforts: one can see how their experimental impulse could provide an aesthetic for the revolutionary fervor of the sixties. But what then is their appeal for the decade that is taking us towards the millennium? One answer may be that they offer an alternative to post-modernism's pose of amnesia. For a climate in which history is just a literary genre, they remind us of the reality of continuity. Against a discourse that insists upon the dissolve of identity – they speak to our sense of community – an interconnecting of artists all wedded to similar projects. To a culture whose key-words are surface and simulation, the Beats respond with a language whose emphasis is on depth and a quest for the authentic.

While contemporary theory celebrates the Death of the Author, the figure of Allen Ginsberg testifies to the importance of keeping him alive. If much of the writing in the nineties examines its own free-floating artifice, that of Ginsberg surfaces from a place that believes its ideas are for real, that its language can be more than the sum of its syntax. Among his chantings and his candor, his naïvety and ambition, can be heard the sound of an America that still yearns to fulfil its own promise – an America whose songs of innocence can be sung by the voice of experience.

# Bibliography

All books are by Allen Ginsberg unless stated otherwise.

**Poetry Books**

*Collected Poems: 1947–1980* HarperCollins, New York, 1984.
*Cosmopolitan Greetings Poems: 1986–1993* HarperCollins, New York, 1994.
*Death & Fame: Poems: 1993–1997* HarperCollins, New York, 1999.
*The Fall of America: Poems of These States* City Lights Books, San Francisco, 1973.
*The Gates of Wrath: Rhymed Poems 1948–1951* Four Seasons, Bolinas, 1972.
*Howl and Other Poems* City Lights Books, San Francisco, 1956.
*Howl Annotated* (with facsimile manuscript) Harper Perennial (paperback), New York, 1995.
*Illuminated Poems* (illustrated by Eric Drooker) Four Walls, Eight Windows, New York, 1996.
*Iron Horse* Coach House Press, Toronto/City Lights Books, San Francisco, 1974.
*Kaddish and Other Poems* City Lights Books, San Francisco, 1961.
*Mind Breaths: Poems 1971–1976* City Lights Books, San Francisco, 1978.
*Planet News* City Lights Books, San Francisco, 1968.
*Plutonian Ode: Poems 1977–1980* City Lights Books, San Francisco, 1982.
*Reality Sandwiches* City Lights Books, San Francisco, 1963.
*Selected Poems: 1947–1995* HarperCollins, New York, 1996.
*White Shroud Poems: 1980–1985* Harper & Row, New York, 1986.

**Photograph Books and Catalogs**

*Allen Ginsberg Photographs* Twelvetrees Press, 1991.
*Snapshot Poetics* Chronicle Books, San Francisco, 1993.

**Prose Books**

*Composed on the Tongue: Literary Conversations 1967–1977* Grey Fox Press, Bolinas, 1980.
*Deliberate Prose: Selected Essays 1959–1995* (edited by Bill Morgan) HarperCollins, New York, 1999.
*Gay Sunshine Interview* (with Allen Young) Grey Fox Press, Bolinas, 1974.
*Indian Journals* Grove Press, New York, 1996.
*Journals: Early Fifties, Early Sixties* (edited by G. Ball) Grove Press, New York, 1977, 1993.
*Journals: Mid-Fifties* HarperCollins, New York, 1995.
*Luminous Dreams* Zasterle Press, Gran Canaria, 1997.
*Selected Interviews* (edited by David Carter) HarperCollins, New York, 1999.
*Straight Hearts' Delight: Love Poems and Selected Letters* (with Peter Orlovsky) Gay Sunshine Press, San Francisco, 1980.
*The Yage Letters* (with William Burroughs) City Lights Books, San Francisco, 1963.

# Index

Page numbers in *italics* refer to illustrations.